I BID YOU FAREWELL

The Life of an Auctioneer

Neil Lanham

First published in 2025 by
Neil Lanham, in partnership with Whitefox Publishing Ltd

www.wearewhitefox.com

EU GPSR Authorised Representative
LOGOS EUROPE, 9 rue Nicolas Poussin, 17000, LA ROCHELLE, France
E-mail: Contact@logoseurope.eu

ISBN 978-1-917523-37-0

Also available as an eBook
ISBN 978-1-917523-38-7

Designed and typeset by Tom Cabot/ketchup
Project management by Whitefox Publishing
Printed and bound by CPI Group (UK) Ltd, Croydon CR0 4YY

The front cover is from a pen and watercolour sketch by Sir John Verney of Neil Lanham taking a sale on 23rd April 1980 at the Town Hall Clare, his happy stamping ground.

Acknowledgements

To my partner Jan Ralling who has checked and rechecked this book and has been a godsend; her full name is Veronica Janice as she was born on VJ night but she is always known as Jan.

To my late wife Hazel Lanham who always stood by me and more than anything believed in me. I have had enormous help and encouragement from Professor John Widdowson without whom I would not have published any academic work at all. Also Margaret Chapman whose humour brought much light relief from the pressures; my old governor Bob Grain for getting me going; my next door solicitor friend Ken Wardle who got me out of more than a few scrapes; John Tasker who was a dependable rock of truth and my Mother Ruby whose advice and help when I stood alone and the need to keep a level head was paramount. And last but not least Alan Samson who has greatly helped to turn this little collection of true lifetime stories of experiences into a book.

CONTENTS

To Rudyard Kipling whose little saying has been of more help to me than I can possibly say:

'I keep six honest serving men (They taught me all I know);
Their names are What and Why and When and How and Where and Who.'

There is a saying that 'the proof of the pudding is in the eating', therefore I have written this book about my life as an auctioneer in three parts:

Chapters 1 to 7: the life that formed 'the pudding'
Chapters 8 to 9: the mixing and ingredients of that 'pudding' and
Chapters 10 to 15: the proving in the eating of 'the pudding'

❀ ❀ ❀ ❀

BY THE SAME AUTHOR:

There's a Story that my Mother Told
and
Wags Aldred Suffolk Stallion Leader

PREFACE

I have always had a curious mind. Curious to the point of rudeness in being a pain in the neck to most people for asking too many questions. It has nevertheless taken me on exciting journeys of discovery. When I was quite young, there lurked – abandoned in an overgrowth of stinging nettles at the rear of the privy at my Grandfather's Red House Farm, Kersey, Suffolk – a very strange contraption. It seemed to haunt me. I had seen nothing like it and my curiosity boiled over. But ask as I may, no one that I spoke to had any knowledge of what it was either.

Again I must have been painful for I was given this contraption to shut me up. I still did not know much about it when I later got it to work and greased it up and took it to an agricultural rally where it was the talk of the weekend and still no one had seen anything like it. I then wrote to the BBC's *Antiques Roadshow*, which requested that I take it along to their event at Layer Marney Tower near Colchester, where a delighted Fiona Bruce ended the show by riding my pedal-drive lawn-roller off into the sunset. My roller was declared unique.

This insatiable curiosity has remained with me all of my life. If I should walk down an old street looking at the houses I know that those with a steep pitched roof were once thatched and those with slated roofs were probably built during the era when the railways

Fiona Bruce on my unique pedal roller.

first arrived. This is just a small part of the interesting and exciting things that lay all around waiting to be observed. When I went out I never wanted to go home, such was the intensity of the things that awaited my observing eye. I feel that this intense curiosity has stood me in good stead as an auctioneer in bringing to light – and fetching record prices – of equally undiscovered items, or 'sleepers' as they are known in the trade.

The title of this book I have taken from a story told to me by Jack Webb, the clerk who had started in 1898 with Mr Charles Boardman at Haverhill in Suffolk. The auctioneer was struggling to get a bid for a poor old cow when a cattle dealer who was getting frustrated at the auctioneer not noticing his bids shouted, "Can I bid, Mr Boardman?" "Of course you can, Bill," came the reply. "Then I bid you farewell," said Bill. As I write in my old age, this saying seems to have an added meaning for me, as at the age of 86, this will surely be my swansong, but before I do bid you farewell I have a story to tell, so please read on.

CHAPTER I

Promotion

"You are going to get promotion, Lanham," said my guvnor, Peter Grain, when he had asked me to go out with him one afternoon. "And there will be a chance of some selling," he added. "You are going to go up to the Machinery Sale with Mr Robert and we will now pay you £5 a week."

You may think that I should have been excited by this prospect but not so. I had been an articled pupil to Mr Peter Grain of the firm of Grain and Chalk, Chartered Auctioneers in Cambridge, for about two out of my three committed years. When this was said to me in 1956, I had become quite depressed at my lack of prospects. Firstly, my widowed mum had signed me up as an articled pupil at no pay, with the partners of this firm asking her for £150 for the privilege. When they found that I was good at drawing plans, I was set up in a tiny top-floor garret at the firm's office in Rose Crescent, Cambridge, to copy plan after plan from the Ordnance Survey.

One day Mr Frank Grain's assistant came up the stairs to my garret saying, "Can you take my car and go and collect some of the firm's For Sale boards that are lying about redundant at properties that we have sold?" I was now 17, had only just passed my driving test, and had not driven anything other than Mother's prewar Morris 8 Tourer but, wanting to do what was expected of me, I reluctantly agreed.

I remember driving along a remote towpath next to the River Cam to collect a board. But the path narrowed, then petered out and I dare not try to turn the car round for fear of it slipping into the river. I nevertheless decided that turning was the only course open to me, and sure enough the car started slipping slowly, slowly down the bank until it came to rest on a muddy plateau about four feet from the flowing river, which would not at this point be shallow. The wheels were now spinning frantically every time that I revved the engine and, worse, the car lurched nearer and nearer to the river edge. I was in despair and desperate and got out of the car to put anything and everything that I could find beneath the back wheels. Nothing seemed to work until at last I came to the For Sale board, that I had collected to use again. The firm had had this especially hand-painted for the job.

I placed it under the wheel, protecting it with some old sacking that I found but this quickly flew off. However, very slowly the wheels gained some traction and I managed to get the car back to the top of the bank – only to discover that the friction from the turning wheels had almost completely obliterated the paintwork on the very board that I had been instructed to collect. I drove back to Cambridge like a dog with its tail between its legs and covered the board with my coat whilst taking it to the basement store of the Rose Crescent office.

Thankfully I saw no one and I then had to struggle singlehanded to put it at the very back of all the other boards in the hope that it would not be discovered for some time – which was the case – and I quietly resumed my plan to keep drawing after this sojourn, as if nothing had happened. On reflecting about this, the whole of my schooldays had been something similar, as I had found myself thinking differently, having different values to most, and I seemed to just escape major punishment at almost every turn. I took more influence from my Mother, who could go back three generations with a continuous flow of stories which carried understandings. At weddings and other hatchings, matchings and dispatchings, I can see her now holding court, with the new generation around her spellbound, as she told them in story after story just who they were.

One day a wealthy farmer's son arrived to share my garret office at Rose Crescent. "I am a pupil, the same as you," he said, "and I have been asked to go and help Mr Robert with the Machinery Sales."

"Well done," I said, "I hope you enjoy it" and I bade him good luck as I knew from reports that he would not find it easy.

Mr Robert's reputation preceded him. He was a tall, handsome ex-army officer who did not suffer fools at all. At the drop of a hat he would lambast anyone and everyone, whoever they may be, who he thought deserved it – and he seemed to think that most people did. Worse than this was the large, corrugated iron shed that he sat in alone, which at sale time became the settling office. It had a doorway but no door at all to the outside, so one was obliged to wear thick clothing and gloves in there all winter.

Almost as bad, but not quite, was the almost undrinkable strong tea, that was made for all who dared drink it by an ancient old boy called Tom Bradley who lived alone with his dog in a caravan down a fen. Tom's tea had a reputation that preceded it. It was so strong that a spoon would almost stand up, and this seemed to be offset by 20 or 30 or more spoonfuls of sugar. Tom did not wash the cups – he scoured them out with wire wool. Needless to say, the wealthy farmer's son did not last the week with Mr Robert and went home to mummy.

Shortly after this yet another pupil with a well-to-do farming father arrived, and he was again promoted over yours truly, a widow's son. He did not even last the week out with Bob Grain, and took off after about two days, never to be seen for over a year. I knew all this as he would occasionally call to see my depressed self at my Rose

Crescent garret room. He would arrive by train from London with large empty suitcases to fill, on his father's account, at Matthews, the old-time grocer's in Trinity Street.

He became a mate and we shared many eccentric moments together, such as when we decided to go ice skating on the ponds up Milton Road, only to find that we were on a sewage farm. Then going on the same evening to see Barry Hardern, another Grain and Chalk employee, who was appearing with his wife in an amateur dramatic show, whilst we were still carrying the whiff of the sewage farm.

My pupil friend somehow acquired a magnificent cream-coloured vintage SS Drophead Jaguar car that he ran on a mixture of paraffin and petrol, and I was always having to help push it to get it started. You sat so low in this thing that you could hardly see over the bonnet. One night we went to a Young Farmers' dance at Ely and when we arrived my suit, clean white shirt and collar was splattered down one

Bob Grain's Machinery Sale – the largest of its kind in Europe.

side with a film of mud off the wheels. Whilst he was away his father sold the car to the local scrap man who cut it up, would you believe, which was not funny. But generally we laughed a lot and it greatly relieved the monotony.

Anyway, when I became the third-choice helper to the infamous Bob Grain I did not consider it to be an honoured promotion, as I was clearly the last hope. I suppose that it was my nervousness that got in the way before that – one of the porters had told me that one of the partners had said, "Be careful with that boy, he's very nervous." I nevertheless did not look the gift horse in the mouth, and although it was for me the last chance saloon, I decided to buckle down to do exactly whatever Mr Robert requested, and try to keep smiling.

There were many stories that went around about Bob Grain and his temper, including the following, true or not I do not know. Apparently an auctioneer had arrived from another firm on sale day and was looking over the auctioneer's shoulder, taking notes on about everything, such as who had entered the lot, what it had realised, and the name of the buyer. Someone told Bob Grain about him, but Grain did not roar at him as might be expected, he quietly sidled up to him saying, "Are you interested in sex and travel?" When the man meekly replied, "I suppose so," this was followed by a very loud, "Well f--- off then."

Mr Robert hardly spoke at all during the first fortnight – a pregnant silence seemed to hang over the place and I wondered if I had jumped out of the frying pan into the fire for, apart from avoiding Tom's tea and observing the scowl on Mr Robert's face as he sipped it, my only job was writing out label after label for Ernie Gilbey, the tractor driver, to attach to each piece of machinery that he was taking to the railway station to be despatched. This is almost 70 years ago but many of the addresses that I laboriously wrote out are still etched into my mind, such as Jim Matten of Mackie Burns, Navan Road, Dublin; and W A Sims, Higher Trevernic, St Columb, Cornwall. But this work, fortunately, did not last forever.

One morning Mr Robert arrived saying, "You'll do some selling in the sale on Monday, Neil." It was the moment that, as an intending auctioneer, I had been waiting for. I should have been highly excited, and I suppose I was deep down, but I was frightened to death and tried hard not to show it. To quote Gregory Peck, "I was about as nervous as a long-tailed cat in a room full of rocking chairs!" My stomach had butterflies every time I thought about it.

"Thank you, sir," I said, "but what shall I do?" Sympathetically he replied, "Always write the price down first or you will forget it, then get the name and initial of the buyer in case they run back, and we have to sue them."

"B-b-but how about the bidding?" I blurted.

"Just go and look to see what other auctioneers do, and practise the increments," he said. "I will put you in Robin Arnold's section at the old pig pens, and tell him that you are to do about 30 lots." I knew Robin well and knew that having gone through the same thing as me, he would be sympathetic to my somewhat pathetic self. Having decided from the start that I would follow whatever Mr Robert said to the T, I set about doing just that.

Neatly piled on the stairs at the Rose Crescent office were packets of new small green valuation books. I duly decided that I was worthy of one and helped myself. In it I wrote every auction saying that I heard, and I went to all the sales that I could, observing how various auctioneers conducted themselves. There was one in Bury St Edmunds who, in his distinct Bury accent, begged people to 'beed' him, and another who had Saturday sales in the Fens, mentioned the bidding umpteen times so it got very boring – he was almost willing people to bid. It was aggressive to the point that if he looked at them and they did not bid he would glare and keep coming back. He would always delay and delay before knocking the hammer down.

Mother knew a very dapper antique dealer called Lloyd Barton who had a small shop in Burwell, and he said that a Mr Britain, a furniture auctioneer of Catlings in Cambridge, was the best. He only mentioned the bidding once and followed this with a pregnant pause, putting the onus on the bidder to get on if he wanted the lot. I went to see him in action. At first I did not agree with his methods, but after much deliberation I saw that his way was by far the best in terms of both speed and obtaining the optimum price, as it made people think that they were going to lose the item.

Furthermore, I realised that the best auctioneers threw their voice to make it as loud as possible. I practised getting my voice to start as low in my stomach as I could so that it had a long way to come out like a foghorn. I thought that I should start the bidding low, encouraging likely bidders to get involved, and then take quick increments. I realised even then that psychology played a big part in auctioneering, and getting the best price came from making people think that they would lose the item.

Of course beneath all the banter you cared deeply. I considered that it would be totally wrong to beg, which gave the impression that no one wanted the lot, and also that this could be a let-down as it gave away that you did not know what it should fetch. It was far better to start low, even if you did this yourself, and let the market in your saleroom take its natural course. You were, in effect, pursuing the optimum. All that flamboyant American style which looked and sounded good, with the auctioneer stringing quick word after word, did little to encourage quick bidding in reality. It owed more to the theatre, I thought. I now firmly believed that to mention the bidding once was the way.

The more that I listened and practised, I found that there is an enormous amount of psychology in disposing of goods at public auction, and this had not reached the 'old school' yet. In later years I was to judge auctioneering competitions for the Royal Institute of Chartered Surveyors. I had now almost filled my green valuation book with all sorts of stock sayings that asked for bids then told the bidders that the bid was theirs, or otherwise, and I practised regularly until I could do it by heart. All this was well before decimalisation, so my practising was in pounds, shillings, and pence, by way of half-crowns and crowns:

"One pound I'm bid. One two and six anywhere?" or, "If you like...?", "May I say...?", "Do I hear...?", "Will you...?" and, if I needed to, then "Last time, all done, the hammer's up", "Going now", "Last time". Bear in mind all that I have said about saying as few words as possible.

Although threatening, one had to give bidders every chance to bid, but quick auctioneers produce quick bidders I was to find, and most people get exasperated with the slow ones. Also I was to discover that if you were making, what seemed to be an extraordinarily good price, you must not show emotion, and must carry on just the same, as if the lot has not yet reached its optimum.

My maths master at school was George Parker and he used to test the class orally by asking, for example, "What is 15 times 7 plus 631" and I had usually been fairly quick to put my hand up. This little exercise taught you to keep three things in your head at once, which was much like auctioneering, where you firstly have to keep in your head the reserve, secondly, the bidding in the saleroom, and thirdly, any price that you may have been asked to bid up to for an absentee. You must never look down at your sale book in mid-flight or you will give the game away that you have probably not yet reached the reserve. You should look only at the bidding public.

It is the same as for most things in life. But had I really prepared myself sufficiently I wondered? This was the real thing and probably my only chance to show what I was made of. The voice of my Uncle Tickles ran loud and clear in my mind, for it was he who had said to me when I was standing back and not taking the responsibility that I should, "Never have it said, boy, that your Mother bred a jibber." A 'jibber' is a standard Suffolk word for someone who is scared and stands back, for a 'jibber' is a horse that is fainthearted and will not go.

Monday came round and Robin handed me the sale book at the agreed lot. I did what Mr Robert had said, but then in my lack of self-belief, I kept trying to hand the sale book back to Robin. But, to my great personal relief, I got through it.

Bob Grain said nothing next morning but later in the week said, "I hear you did alright, Neil. Next sale I will put your name in the catalogue and you will sell the whole section."

Nervous was not the word – I could not sleep.

The sale morning came round, and I remember that I was sitting on a seat in the public toilets when I heard the porter sound the bell for the start of my section. I hastily gathered my trousers and the sale book, in that order, and hurried to where the sale of Lot 1 was to take place. After a few words about the highest bidder to be the buyer ("Unless anyone bids more!" – I have sometimes said this to relax my audience, but I could afford no frivolity on this very important occasion) and a few more short quick statements about clearing of the goods, I started the auction and never looked back. I sold about the first 200 lots in my miscellaneous section with no fuss and I was feeling really proud of myself.

I was about to start on the tractor wheels section when a pupil that I knew from the firm's Royston office, came up saying that his manager had told him to come and take over from me. I knew nothing of this and indeed it was my name that Mr Robert had put as the auctioneer in the catalogue. However, I handed him the sale book as he had requested. It was quite fortuitous that I did not depart immediately, because I soon heard a row and raised voices coming from where my colleague was selling.

On approaching the argument that was going on I asked my colleague, "What's the matter?" He replied, "This man says that he bid £18 and this man also says that he bid £18, so which one shall I let have it?" Realising that he had lost control, I took the sale book back from him, taking the bid of £18 from one of them and telling the other that he would have to bid more if he was interested. The other protested of course, but was still bidding at £25 when I knocked the lot down to him. Of course they both wanted the lot at this seemingly low price and were taking my colleague for a ride.

The next morning, the incident had obviously reached the guvnor for he asked me what the kerfuffle had been about. So I told him that the Royston office manager had told his lad to take over. I imagined the telephone line when Bob Grain got to speaking to the Royston manager. I'll bet he stopped his chortling in church. The big lesson was that there can only be one person in charge – the auctioneer – who should seamlessly conduct the proceedings impartially and in quiet control, as does a good football referee.

At Cambridge market, on Machinery Sale days, there would be all sorts of side stalls and one needed to beware of scams. One man's ploy was to say, "Who wants to buy a pound note for sixpence?" He would have about five pound notes laid on his counter, upon which he would put each person's sixpence. Then he would say to the first person, "Now you have twenty shillings and sixpence, but for a further ten shillings you can have that glass jug and tumblers." Then he would say, "For a further pound you can have so-and-so, and if there is anything else you like say so" and before he had finished the punter had shelled out about £5 or £6 for a load of toot. Then he would go along the line with the other pound and sixpence that he had laid out, selling all goods that looked cheap but were not.

On this particular day a big lorry driver in his singlet, with a deep shining tan and bulging muscles, was at the end of the line, and after the stallholder's spiel he said, "I'll just take my pound please."

"Oh no no no!" said the stallholder. "You can have this and that and…"

"If you don't give me the money as you said you would, you'll feel the weight of these fists." With no further ado, the red-faced spuffler, with great reluctance, handed Mr Muscles his pound and sixpence.

I BID YOU FAREWELL

There was a man selling Swiss watches out of a suitcase. In the immediate years preceding the war it was impossible to buy things such as Swiss watches in British shops. With the many restrictions that applied they had to be smuggled in. The man's spiel was, "I am not asking £30, not even £20 but just £10 for this very valuable watch. Now who wants it?" When someone said, "I do," he would say, "Now just a minute I have a better offer for you" and he would lay the £10 and the watch side by side in one of his hands saying, "Now there is the £10 there and the watch worth another ten at least. Will you give me £15 for the two?" I actually saw a punter shell out £15 for his own £10 back and the watch. Unbelievable – I would not have believed it if I had not seen it with my own eyes.

Apart from the week of the Machinery Sales, on Mondays I would be with Mr Peter Grain at the market selling the fat cattle, and my job generally was to run sheets of entries to the office where the booking in of the cattle took place. When we started selling, I would stand next to Peter Grain to take the weight of each beast from a massive machine. On all maiden heifers and all steers there was a subsidy, but if there was any doubt about the heifers being maiden they would be rejected by the ministry graders. There were dealers there who if they did not agree with the grader, would buy the beast and present it at another grading centre. If a heifer was in doubt about being maiden the old drovers/porters knew and would shout "Been to the whist drive sir, been to the whist drive."

Life had completely changed for me from my Rose Crescent garret days. I had a regular girlfriend, a farmer's daughter named Brenda, and together with another Grain and Chalk pupil, Tony Mullocks and his girlfriend, we had treated ourselves to tickets for the legendary May Ball at Trinity College, Cambridge, which was an all-night affair with Scottish, Calypso and English dance bands. We were then going to punt to the renowned Grantchester tea rooms for breakfast.

PROMOTION

I felt a bit like my guvnor's blue-eyed boy now. However, I have always found that when everything has started to be too good to be true, that is the time that it will start to go wrong. True enough – when I arrived one morning I was addressed by a porter, "You wait till the guvnor sees you – you are really for it." He reminded me that I had taken a phone message from the main office about four o'clock the previous afternoon that I was to tell Mr Robert that the store cattle that were coming from Ireland had arrived, and he was to take his workforce and collect them from the nearby station immediately. I remember that something had happened, then something else, and I had gone home at 5.30pm without delivering this extremely important message to the guvnor, who was setting out the sale ground for lots down the bottom meadow. I could not believe that I had done this and feared that it could be a sackable offence, for the cattle had remained on the train all night without water.

Fortunately Bob Grain was still setting out the far meadow, but I knew a message for him would arrive sooner or later and I would have to deliver it and confront him. About 12 noon that message arrived, and I took it to where he was. Standing well back – for I had no idea how he would take my immense misdemeanour – I delivered the new message. Obviously I looked distraught but all that he said was, "Neil did you forget about the cattle?" I tried to reply how sorry I was but before I could he said, "Forget about it." To this day I always get a lump in my throat when I think of how that hard-bitten, short-tempered man had let me off so lightly.

Although I thoroughly appreciated what he had done for me, he was always Mr Robert and I could not find myself to have enough confidence to talk to him as I would like to have done, and show my appreciation. When in later life I had antique sales, he came, bringing his French wife, who was incidentally also an agricultural machinery dealer, and Mike Mitcham and David Over. Mitcham's, I believe, were the largest second-hand farm machinery dealers in this country at that time.

I BID YOU FAREWELL

I still could not relax enough to speak to Mr Robert on an equal level. How stupid! I now bitterly regret that I did not show him my appreciation for taking me out of the quagmire and putting me on the road to success. He was the only one who had given me any under-standing and confidence, and I truly believe that if it had been left to anyone else they would not have given me a cat in hell's chance. I think that part of the reason that I got on so well with the bad-tempered Mr Robert was that both my Grandfather on Mother's side and my Uncle Tickles had tempers that flew at the drop of a hat, and I had established in my mind that the only thing that you could do is to say nothing if possible – but if you have to speak then say only the truth, and if they asked you to do something that was impossible, stand up to them and quietly tell them so, and then get out of the way as soon as possible.

My Mother always had a great interest in horses and much later in life had bought a lame foal at Tattersalls sales in Newmarket. It eventually went to Dicky Westbrook to be trained and with our twins, my wife Hazel and I took my Mother to see it win the Richard Marsh Handicap for her at Newmarket Racecourse in 1984. On the way to lead her winner in, I just had time to introduce Mother to the gentleman that had stood next to us in the stands – Bob Grain.

To be fair it had not been too bad at Grain and Chalk's when I first arrived in 1954. Well! Apart from the first day when I was told that we were going to measure some land. That's okay I thought, expecting that we would use a tape measure. Not so. I was to discover that we were to use a chain. A chain is made of metal and has a hundred links, measuring 22 yards in total, with a brass open handle at each end. It is the length of a cricket pitch. In this modern world of metric measures such as the metre etc., a chain is absolutely ancient, although it is still the basis on which our knowledge of pre-metric measurement stands.

To drag a chain over ploughed land in wet weather is an appalling thing to have to do, for it grabs at the wet soil and one is soon dragging hundredweights of congealed mud. I was exhausted after only a few minutes and went home that night with a sort of cramp in my legs that caused the rest of my foot to flap uncontrollably. Every split-second I longed to get home, but to no avail.

I survived this, only to be told that we were going to lot-up a farm live and dead stock auction on the next day. We arrived at the farm and the rain poured and poured in bucketsful, straight down, full-bore. It ran off my cap over my bare neck down the inside of my shirt and out the bottom, having wetted me everywhere. My white riding mackintosh became a saturated sort of greyish-yellow. It was not cold, and somehow I enjoyed it. Having been well groomed in the 'Kersey farming tradition' by my Uncle Tickles when I had worked at Grandfather's Suffolk farm, in my egotism I felt that I knew more about it than these 'townies' of office background. I could and did bear the pain in a strange macho fashion. The old boys on Grandfather's farm who never stopped for a thing such as rain, would have been proud of me, I thought.

There was another pupil named Robert at Grain and Chalk's when I arrived, who was in his last year and he showed me the ropes, such as buying our lunchtime cheese or ham and butter from Sainsbury's. At that time they had long marble-topped counters on either side of the shop, where he invariably got in an argument with some old dear who would accuse him of jumping the queue.

Sainsbury's, then in St Andrew's Street, was the last of a dying breed of shops that, when one tendered the cash, it was despatched in a screw-top container via an elasticated wire-pull system, that roared one's cash in haste over everyone's head to a lady cashier sitting in an elevated position in the far corner of the shop, who would then return your change and receipt!

I well remember my mum phoning the office with the important news that this branch was selling Argentine rib of beef at 7p a pound – would I please get some on the way home?

Unless very busy, Robert and I would go out of the office for mid-morning coffee to Matthews, opposite Trinity College, where there were white damask tablecloths on the tables. Robert had labelled it the 'old maid's paradise'. If we had nothing on at all and no one would know, we would spend the afternoon at the Odeon picture house. On one occasion we sat almost next to the office manager Miss Brenda Taylor and her boyfriend on her day off. Brenda Taylor was nice but strict, and commanded respect as she kept the whole place ticking over. Robert also kept admonishing yours truly for wearing my cap on the back of my head and not over my eyes as he had perfected.

After Robert left, Terry Peterson arrived from Hertfordshire. He was an avid cricket fan and played for his village team. We would either spend our lunchtimes at the place where apparently cricketers congregated – you've guessed The Cricketers Pub – or we would take our Sainsbury's grub to Fenners, the University Cricket ground, and watch the likes of the emerging Ted Dexter play. Dexter went on to captain his country. Terry did not stay long at all, and when later stooges likewise quickly departed I got fed up with just plan drawing, and eating bread and 'pull-it' on my own.

It would be totally wrong however for me to pass any reflections on Cambridge itself as I loved the place, and still do. It has so many facets, virtues, and interesting places. I remember as a kid of five, going with my mum to visit my dad in Addenbrooke's Hospital, which was then situated in what seemed like a very large house in Trumpington Street.

I also remember I had been scolded for treading in a stream of water that progressed along the gutter. This I later learned was called Hobson's Conduit, and had been installed by Thomas Hobson in 1610–14, to run in the gutters as an ever-flowing stream throughout the centre of Cambridge, thus keeping the town clean. The same man gave his name to 'Hobson's Choice', a saying meaning that you had no choice, for he was what was known as a 'job master', letting out horses for the day. If you went to him, you had to take the next available horse, so you had no choice at all, hence the expression. I used to bolt down my Sainsbury's bread and cheese so that I could go exploring this interesting place in the rest of my lunchtime.

Also along Trumpington Street was the Fitzwilliam Museum that housed things such as international art and Rodin's bronze *The Kiss*. Work by almost every artist of any importance is kept there, and ancient artefacts likewise. Nearby were many other museums, each on its own separate subject, such as the Whipple Museum of Measurement. The importance of clear and accurate measurement being a fad of mine, I could dwell there forever. Also not far away was the Polar Research Institute with details of Scott's fatal and pathetic attempt to reach the North Pole.

Along nearby Downing Street was the Anthropology Museum where I enjoyed reading about the Pitt River Expedition. My Grandfather on my father's side, George Lanham, had been on this expedition to Benin, where he caught malaria, which made him only fit to serve as a coastguard afterwards. The only post then available to him was at Donagadee in Northern Ireland, in the midst of the Troubles. Here he was put up against a wall to be shot but somehow escaped. I remember him well as he always had a story for me about how he used to ride on crocodiles' backs in far off lands and how he eventually got rid of a frog that had jumped down his throat while he was asleep. They say that we are all as we are because of our past, and I do believe that such things influenced how I act similarly now with my own children.

Almost next to the Anthropology Museum was the place where Crick and Watson had discovered the double helix of life. Then off Regent Street there was a park known as Parker's Piece where reputedly football under rules was first played (Cambridge Rules). Here the famous England cricketer Jack Hobbs learned his trade and I remember standing next to him when he coached at my old school.

The Cambridge Folk Festival was about the biggest and best in the country. Here I saw Paul Simon from the USA, and many other famous names, including Sydney Carter, who had just written 'Lord of the Dance'. Then a bit further along in Trumpington Street there were the Botanical Gardens, which were then free, and I would go there to eat my ploughman's. In the Gardenia, a Greek restaurant in Rose Crescent, at the cellar bar Mario would come in and get everyone doing Zorba's dance. There was traditional jazz at the Rex Ballroom, and modern ballroom dancing every Saturday night at The Dorothy was a legend.

At the start of King's Parade was a café where one could get a coffee and gaze across at the Senate House, designed by James Gibbs, a contemporary of Sir Christopher Wren, no less. Its proportions are so perfect that it gives me palpitations even now, as does one of his other designs, St Paul's Cathedral. From the sublime to the ridiculous, in the centre of the Market Square was a downstairs gentleman's toilet with full-time attendant in white flannels, who daily polished the brass throughout, including all pennies in the slot machines. No wonder the spies Anthony Blunt and co. loved it!

In the colleges one walked on paths that had been trodden by many famous people. Those that I was later to appreciate for their wisdom concerning measurement were Charles Darwin, who said that he "put away books to discover wisdom with his hands"; the electrical genius Lord Kelvin who had passed through his college as a teenager and who said, "Where there is no measurement there is no understanding"; and the mathematician Sir Isaac Newton, who said similar words.

Having succeeded with the gavel I was now feeling that perhaps I could make it as an auctioneer after all. I found a bit more spring in my step and I now looked forward to the events that would determine my future.

CHAPTER 2

A Pupil's Lot

On reflection I think that we made the right decision for me to become an auctioneer. At school I had always been a bit of a budding entrepreneur. My father had died when I was just five years old, and I think that this had affected me more than

The author using his loaf.

anyone then would believe. My determined Mother had scrubbed floors to get a start in her hired boarding house to make up for our loss. Father had done some estimates for the installation of electricity at Kimbolton School and had died with the thought that he wanted me to be educated there, and Mother's determination was such that she would die rather than let him down.

For some reason I had become withdrawn and almost mute and nervous of people. I seemed to have gone backwards and had four schools in three years. The only place that I found solace was with the older farm workers 'down the cart lodge' of Grandfather's farm and I learned to love their steady countenance.

Mother had seemed delighted to get me into Kimbolton School, and being a widow the powers that be had been generous with a reduced fee. But I was not so sure when I entered firstly as a boarder at under eight years old. At school the only thing that I excelled in was art, but unbeknown to me my art master, Donald Hood-Cree – who had studied at the Slade in London and in Paris – had been to see Mother with the suggestion that I should be taken away from Kimbolton School and sent to an art college. She must have sent him away with a flea in his ear because the next picture that I took to show him, thinking that it was my best yet, he mercilessly crabbed, leaving me feeling totally deflated and crestfallen. It took away what little confidence I had, for I now had nothing at which I could shine. It is only recently that the penny has dropped as to what happened and it has made me wonder how far I might have got as an artist.

For instance, Mother as a girl had hunted with the Essex and Suffolk Foxhounds, and so had Sir Alfred Munnings, who she got to know quite well. She met him again watching horses train on the heath at Newmarket and asked him round for a cup of tea. "Who did that," he said of the head of a farm horse that I had painted, and then said, "What is he doing now?"

"He is working on his Grandfather's farm," Mother said, to which he replied, "Wasting his time. He can paint the head and ears as well as I can." But it was to be all in vain.

Furthermore, my Uncle Tickles, Mother's younger brother, who also worked on Grandfather's farm, gave me an unexpected lecture about this time saying, "Them old artists don't make no money, boy. You are good at saving your money and you'd better by half do something in business." He was right about saving money because, following Father's death, we had almost none, and all I now wanted to do was be a farmer. Grandfather huffed and puffed about allowing me to have a few acres to start a breeze block piggery, but Mother had wintered and summered him and knew that he would never come up with the rhino for anyone other than himself.

To be fair to him, although he had said, "He will never be any good as long as he has a hole up his... you know where," he also went on to say, "If he can save a hundred pounds, I'll give him another hundred." I was determined not to be beaten and set myself out to prove it. To raise this first hundred became a challenge and I did it by dealing at school in anything I could, such as selling second-hand comics, and now that I was a dayboy I could sell half my midday sandwich lunch to seemingly well-off boarders. Sweets were still on ration then and my best line was in buying unwanted sweet coupons from grown-ups and converting them into PK chewing gum, which I could sell at school, off ration, at double the price to the well-heeled boarders. On a very wet sports afternoon that was rained off, I took ten shillings, which was immense in the circumstances.

I would deal in almost anything. I had a competitor in Boris, a sort of insignificant, thin, spotty-faced boarder who you would have thought dare not say boo to a goose. What he would do was save all his tuck then raffle it off, moving from classroom to classroom with his fruit and sweets displayed in a flat box. One break he came into our classroom displaying his wares and saying his usual patter. He got about halfway through this when he suddenly noticed that a master was seated quietly behind the door where he had not been observed. "What have got there, Boris?" said the master who had realised his little game. He then proceeded to throw Boris's hard saved goods around the classroom saying, "A pear for you Peacock, bananas for you Smith, a Cox's orange pippin for me," giving something to each boy whilst Boris stood crestfallen and totally deflated.

Luckily I never got caught and I had up my sleeve an even better money-making ploy if only I could work it. Mother wanted to buy a house in Newmarket as it was nearer to her old Suffolk home, and with her love of all things to do with horses, as a family we used to take a fair bit of interest in horseracing. Now the Derby was coming up, and I was in luck's way, for it was to be held on the same date as the School Sports Day, which meant that the whole school would be sitting outside on benches and I would be able to move around quite easily. During the month leading up to my money-making adventure, I had made a few small ante-post bets on some of the favourites with bookmakers in order to spread the risk. On the day I laid odds to my punters that were just a bit less than the probable starting prices. As I could not get round to all the school, I asked my mate Mick Leach to come in with me and away we went, moving from bench to bench around all those in the school who might be interested in a punt. Someone had a portable radio, so we soon found out which horse had won – it was a horse called Tulyar ridden by Charlie Smirke. Tulyar was about fifth or sixth favourite, and would you believe it, not one boy had backed it. It was a raucous time as we counted our ill-gotten gains on the school bus going home.

We lived very frugally in these years immediately after the war, and when Mother came home with the local dental mechanic's demob suit that she had bought for a pound I winced, for it had wide pinstripe lapels, turn-ups and padded shoulders, when at school strictly only plain grey was worn. Mother had cut bits out and tightened it up where necessary, and although I got ribbed by some boys who guessed its origin, I never did receive the expected tap on the shoulder.

In terms of rations, I did not eat steak until I was over 21, so perhaps Uncle Tickles was right, the principle here being that if you have never personally known a particular thing how can you miss it? What I mean is that during the war years we had neither bananas nor sherbet. I heard people talk about them but not having known them I could not conceive what they were and therefore did not miss them. That is how people who were labelled as poor got by, the principle being again if you have never experienced it then how can you miss it?

At school it was compulsory that all eligible boys joined the CCF – the Combined Cadet Force. If not you had to go into the Pioneer Corps which was something like being a conscientious objector and no one wanted that. When it was nearing the end of term and my schooling all together, we were advised that an Air-Vice Marshall was coming to inspect the troops and witness a mock invasion demonstration, and that thunder-flashes would be issued. I knew from past experience that this would not include me. I was an outsider and a rebel who they knew had difficulty in conforming to all these pretend toy soldier games, and although I was a marksman and proudly wore the cross-rifle badge on my arm, I had never been asked to represent the school at shooting or in anything else for that matter. For this mock invasion I therefore arranged my own mock weapons in addition to the issued blanks for my .303 rifle. I had a .22 starter's pistol and some loud bangers that Uncle Tickles had left over from scaring crows. We were stationed in some long grass where I thought that I could not be seen. However although about a field away our CO, Fred Langley, became exceedingly interested in these very different bangs I was letting off, and unbeknown to me had his binoculars trained on yours truly. No one said anything, as I was leaving school soon, but I got some very strange looks from Fred Langley whilst we were clearing up. If you were to ask me now why I did it I would simply say 'boredom'. Bored at not being able to do the things that counted in my book and frustration at having to take part in theirs – or as Winston Churchill put it, "My education was only interrupted by my schooling." Or as Mark Twain said, "I was educated once and it took me years to get over it." As you may have guessed in ploughing my own furrow I have spent a lifetime collecting quotes of reason from the great men who have gone before.

I only obtained two GCE O-levels, and even failed my beloved art which I feel tells you how dejected I had become. I did, however, win the boy's prize for fishing on the River Ouse at St Neots.

But now that I knew what I was to do for my living, and realising what my 'education' to afford this was costing my poor old mum, I strove a bit more to achieve exam results and at the following winter sitting I obtained the necessary English and two more subjects.

Mother had saved all she possibly could and in 1952 bought a large house at Newmarket that needed a lot of doing up. In fact what had happened was that during the war Grandfather made a killing and did not know what to do with his money. Like nearly all farmers before the war he had nothing – not two 'hapeth' to rub together, and had a dog tied up everywhere (Mother's way of saying unpaid bills!). But now, said Mother, he was as rich as a sheeny. There had been a bad depression on the land in the '30s, a time of which Mother said, "If you had nothing you were lucky, for you hadn't got the worry of losing it, because as sure as god made little green apples, that was what would happen." These stories of hardship left a marked impression on me and I began my business life in the fear that they could happen again. The wheat quota had helped, but farmers were still struggling.

When war broke out in 1939 the new standing army wanted beer. Beer comes from malt and malt from barley and as fortune would have it Grandfather had most of his 280 acres down to barley that year. The corn was cut then put into shocks and then stacks as usual, ready to be threshed out with the Marshall threshing drum when it was due to leave the farm. The price of barley then went up and up and up and Grandfather just sat and sat and sat and waited. The price was ridiculous, and barley was getting like gold dust. When Grandfather did thresh it out, according to Uncle Tickles, the barley had overheated and turned black in the stack, but the maltsters were so desperate for it that they still took it as there was nothing being imported in these early days of the war when the German U-boats ruled the seas.

This meant that Grandfather now did not know what to do with all his money. Desperate to avoid the 'all in one year' policy of the tax man, the bank manager confidentially advised depositing the money in the accounts of his sons and daughters, and this included £2,000 to my Mother Ruby's account, which gave her the wherewithal to help buy the Newmarket house. Despite all the bad times she had been through with her father – 'the old man' – when she worked his land for no or little pay she had not touched his money that lay in her account but now she really needed it and told him so, at which he quaked, but then reluctantly agreed. In reality Mother had earned it off her father many times over when he could not pay her in the bad years, as when the bailiffs put stickers on their furniture and kept sending notices "That unless…"

Mother and I went to see Merrick Griffiths, the Newmarket auctioneer that she had met when furnishing her flats, to ask his advice about me becoming a rural auctioneer. "I think that Peter Grain is the man to speak to," he said and phoned him there and then. Peter Grain was the senior partner in the prestigious agricultural firm of Grain and Chalk of Cambridge, and we then made arrangements for me to meet him at his Rose Crescent office. I had seen him on the rostrum when I had gone with Uncle Tickles to see his horse sold at the Cambridge horse sales. There are many pitfalls in buying a horse, for there is much that can go wrong. Uncle Tickles pointed out to me a horse that had a load of mud over its hooves, and said that this had been put there to cover up a swelling on a bad foot. He also explained how the old horse dealers would 'ginger up' a horse by putting a piece of ginger up its rear end which would make it come into the ring quite sprightly. There was also what they called 'Puffin the glins', one of many tricks that were done to make them look younger.

Anyway, we had found out some important news that if I attended the College of Estate Management in St Albans Grove, Kensington, for three terms I could take the first two parts of the Chartered Auctioneers' exam at the same time. My absence from Grain and Chalk for three short terms was agreed. Mother even arranged lodgings for me with her old Suffolk friend Ethel Philo at 2 Eridge Road, Chiswick, W8, for three pounds, five shillings a week, and found that the West Suffolk Education Authority would pay towards my education fee. My sister Audrey was now teaching and with a friend.

Mother drove me up to London and with much difficulty found 2 Eridge Road and I was deposited there. The next day was open day at the college, and I duly walked down to Turnham Green tube station to take the 'Green Line' to High Street Kensington. I took a short cut through Barkers Store to arrive at the college in St Albans Grove, then mooched around all day speaking to virtually no one other than when I went to get a cup of tea in the basement café. When I went to get on the tube to go back to Chiswick I found that three trains had independently arrived, one after the other, and departed Kensington High Street Station, and I had not even got on the platform. I turned round to get out of this throng of pushers and walked dejectedly up Kensington Church Street where I remembered that someone had told me to take a 27 bus to Chiswick High Road. At last one came along and I got on board only to find that I did not have a clue where to get off. It seemed to me to be almost an offence to speak to anyone in London and I think that the bus was halfway to Barnes before I got off, having then to find my way back to Chiswick and then across past Turnham Green, to arrive exhausted at Eridge Road.

At supper I met the other two lodgers. One, Bob Philp, an amiable Scottish lad who worked at the Tax Office, asked me if I was going home at the weekend. "If I do," I said, "I fear that I may not be coming back." At 17 this was only my second visit to the great metropolis, and I had difficulty coping. Bob could see that I was crestfallen and said, "Come on let's go and find some buses." He knew all the routes around the city and we found that if I walked across Kensington Gardens and past the Round Pond featured in Peter Pan, I could then catch an 88 bus along Bayswater Road, through Shepherd's Bush and Goldhawk Road, and I could then get off in Acton and walk to Eridge Road and it would be quicker. After that I mainly travelled in London by bus and en route got to enjoy looking at some of the places that I had only heard of before.

The next day was better. At the lectures I took I met students of a like interest, including my old mate Bob Cheek from the Isle of Wight, who I usually still see at least once a year, and, with Dave Wood from Carlisle, who was also on the same rural auctioneers' course, we became a sort of 'Trois Amigos'.

My allotted personal tutor was a Mr Biles who was religious, and took the valuations course which was our main subject. Valuations, I was to discover were not about guessing, but estimating the rental value, then capitalising it according to the risk factor. It strongly featured arithmetic, so it was one of my better subjects. Biles was a stickler for time and if you arrived one minute late you were expelled from his lecture room immediately. I made a point of being on time, but one morning about halfway through the term, I arrived about five minutes late. I quietly entered expecting to be turned out but to my mates' astonishment all Biles said was, "Oh! Go and sit down." Had I found another Fairy GodMother as I had in Bob Grain? Perhaps so, and after this I worked to please him, coming second in the whole of the college in the end of term examination. Why I appreciated these little compliments so much, I feel, is that they were so few and far between.

On another occasion, the Agricultural Professor put me down on a point in front of the class. These academics, I found, had no or little hands-on experience in agriculture, as I had had with Uncle Tickles, and I did not rate them. I smarted in defeat and looked up the point and found that I was right. I told my colleague Bob. "I would not say anything if I were you," said Bob, "for he sets and marks the exam papers." Good advice I thought, for as I went through life I discovered that there are many times that you know that you are right in a confrontation, but to win you need to let the other side feel that they are correct when they are not. Ego is a very strong thing, and I was to discover how important it was in the psychology of selling.

Dave Wood said that he would like to go to the London University Ball at the Festival of Britain Hall on the South Bank. He knew a girl called Jo from home who was at a girls' college, and she said that she could find Bob and I partners. It was a great night dancing to Little Sid Phillips on his clarinet in front of his well-known orchestra. We even had a burlesque dancer who semi-stripped. I remember how all the lads clapped and shouted "more" but one wag shouted "less" – meaning her clothing, I suppose! After the dance we went back to the three girls' nearby flat for a coffee.

In the college holidays I went back to work at Grain and Chalk and by the end of my London sojourn had passed all exams, apart from the final which I was to take in two years' time.

When not working with Mr Robert Grain I would help Mr Frank who was one of Mr Robert's younger brothers in charge of the firm's farms for sale in East Anglia. He dressed the part always wearing a thorn-proof tweed suit and heavy 'Zug Veltshoen' pimpled brown shoes. Like Mr Robert he was quick, to the point, and did not suffer fools gladly. I remember waiting for him whilst we were late for an appointment to take on a farm for sale. He was selling another farm on the phone and drinking a cup of coffee down at the same time in one gulp. He asked me one day to draw some plans of a farm for which he had drawn up the schedule. I noticed that he had made a mistake, so I milked the occasion for all that it was worth by sounding a long "Aah!" to which he replied "What is it? What is it?" I then took my time in pointing out that in the middle of a field was a separate tiny plantation that had its own Ordnance Survey number. This was rare and he had missed it.

On another occasion when I was getting fed up with just drawing plans and colouring the copies, I knocked on his door, then went in and frankly told him that I was a bit pissed off. "Go and get your hat, boots and coat," he instantly said. "We are going to take details for a farming stock auction." Yippee, I thought, I have cracked it. We then proceeded to the farm where he told me to write each lot on a separate line in a valuation book. This meant that you could transfer the lots in the order that you wanted them in the catalogue by putting a mark down the side of each lot as you transferred it, so that nothing would get missed. The order of sale would probably start with the customary heap of scrap iron, then to make sure that every lot, particularly the miscellanea, was listed in order so that one could proceed in line without any deviation as the auctioneer went round on the day of sale. When one moved on to the farm implements and machinery, one should then get them in the same order as one would use them during the various seasons. After the miscellanea one should therefore start with the ploughs, then the manure spreaders, harrows, cultivators, drills, tractors, ending up with the combine or harvesting equipment. This was absolutely what I wanted. I got as far as I could before time came for me to catch my train home. The next morning, bright-eyed and bushy-tailed, I knocked on his door as soon as I got in, excited about carrying on, only to be told by himself that he had finished it the previous night. I did not hear from him again, and returned to my garret as highly deflated as when I had knocked on his door.

Interestingly, when he retired he spent the next five years catching eels at Ely with fyke nets and selling them alive to Dutch fish merchants. I went to see him once in his old age with my video camera and he then sat in a chair all day making nets by hand for almost any purpose. He also told many tales about his poaching exploits. Apparently all that he had ever wanted to be was a poacher. Like myself he had been a pupil of his uncle, Peter Grain, who was a foxhunting man and when Frank had been caught poaching and he was to come up before the bench he was scared to death of Mr Peter finding out.

The Grains, as a family, came from Ely. Mr Peter's brother was Mr Henry whose sons were Frank, Robert and John. John was in charge of the Ely office of A T Grain and Sons. He had an irascible old porter called Nibby Lee who everyone loved as he was always up to mischief. The first week that I arrived we had a house contents sale in conjunction with the Ely office. Lunchtime was spent in the local pub, where one was obliged to keep pace with alcoholic refreshments in this macho world. I realised too late that it was Nibby's idea to get the young pupils addled, and when Mr Frank's wife came to view she spoke to me and I had not a clue what I was saying. Henry and all his sons were boxers and represented their local Ely club. Having short tempers they had been known to cause a few ructions.

The Chalk's side of the firm was run from an office off St Andrews Street. Many were the tales told about Tom Chalk's bad memory. He would get a lift into Cambridge with his daughter then, when it was time to go home, complain to the police that his car had been stolen. On one occasion a very important arbitration was to be held at Tom's office. The farmer whose land the arbitration was about arrived early, so Tom said "Would you wait in here please?" and put him in a room on his own. Everyone else duly arrived and waited and waited. Then as the farmer had not appeared they went home. Much later an irate farmer was discovered where Tom had put him.

My three years of pupillage at Grain and Chalk had elapsed and I now needed a job. Whilst I could stay with Bob Grain indefinitely it seemed, I needed experience in all the aspects of the profession. Positions in the agricultural auctioneering profession that I sought were generally advertised in the *Estates Gazette*, so I scanned this each week. Most positions required someone with more experience than myself, but I secured interviews at Ekins Witherow and Handley, which ran St Ives Market, and Lacy Scott of Bury St Edmunds, where my lack of more general experience let me down. I think that if it had been left to Henry Lacy Scott I would have got the job, but John, who I was to brush with later on, seemed to take delight in exposing what he seemed to think were my weaknesses.

Mother drove me up to Atherstone in the Midlands for an interview with John Briggs and Calder, which ran two markets. I enjoyed the interview and felt that I could have been offered the job, but on reflection was not too keen on going into the industrial Midlands, when agriculture was my first love. Calder asked me about my outside interests and when I told him that I was treasurer of the local Young Conservatives, he said that they would not approve of any political involvement. I had not thought about it as political. If so I would not have told him, but the Young Conservatives to me was just somewhere for young people to go, and we avoided all politics as far as possible. If anything I was the other way inclined as I very much associated myself with the struggle of the old boys on the land who had befriended me at Grandfather's farm. Since then I have always tried to be absolutely independent on all political matters and keep any thoughts thereon to myself. Some of the people that I was to rub shoulders with were even communists, but so what? The thing of primary importance to me was the job and I put that first to a fault. My personal problem being that I did not always see the people in between.

I felt disappointed not to have been offered the job as assistant at Spurlings and Hempson, which had the Tuesday Market in Ipswich.

I got on well with the senior partner, Leonard Hempson, and met his younger partner Charles Lowe, who had been at my old school. When I learned that I was not to be offered this position I was considering taking a post that I had been offered as an assistant to the County Land Agent at Ipswich. They were particularly interested in my plan drawing but I knew that I would miss the auctioning, which I took a real pride in, so I was not really keen. I think that the worst thing for me about this time was that I had lost my girlfriend Brenda. It was all over a stupid dispute about me apparently invariably arriving late. I was in a miserable state for a while, but what happened next helped a lot.

CHAPTER 3

Happy Days Out East

Out of the blue came a handwritten letter from a Mr Michael Spear, who said that his father had recently died. With his unqualified uncle, he ran a weekly cattle market at Campsey Ashe near Woodbridge in East Suffolk, from a general practice in Wickham Market nearby. I showed Mother his letter and her reply was, "Let's go and have a look on Sunday." My sister Audrey drove us down in her recently acquired Austin Atlantic – a very smart car for a schoolteacher, I thought, but did not look a gift horse in the mouth.

We met Michael, then we looked at the market which was very much smaller than the one that I was used to in the great metropolis of Cambridge, but there was something about the unstated smallness of this place that I liked. Apparently Michael's Grandfather had opened the market in the 1920s and they now sold about 40 fat cattle and 350 fat pigs a week as well as almost anything and everything that a country market could sell. Pigs were sold as either porkers, cutters or baconers – porkers were about six score in weight (a score being 20 pounds) and cutters seven score. The idea was that Michael sold the cattle and the fat pigs, and I would sell about everything else, which would be the fat sows, store pigs, poultry, game, furniture, produce and timber. Apparently Michael had been an articled pupil to Leonard Hempson of Ipswich, as I had been to Mr Peter Grain, and on the death of his father he had sought his old employer's advice and was given the file on his recent advertisement for an improver. Roger Pasco had got the job. I knew Roger as he had worked for F G Parker of Mildenhall, which had a pig auction in Cambridge Market. I must have been the next best to Roger. Michael Spear seemed desperate, as his partner, Uncle Claude, had completely lost his voice upon the death of his brother.

After inspecting the market, Mother said, "I think that this is for you, boy." So it was agreed that I would start as soon as Grain and Chalk would release me. I would be paid £675 a year as a not yet fully qualified improver. Michael strongly recommended that I took lodgings with his Mother, Norah Spear, at the Beeches in Melton. He said that she got on well with young people and needed the company. She was, however, still holidaying with another son, Robin, in Canada following the death of her husband Donald, who had been the senior partner. Norah would not be back for two or three weeks so I could stay with Michael, his wife Margaret, and their two young girls until Norah returned. Michael lived in a fine bungalow that he had had built among the trees at Great Bealings near Woodbridge. He said that he would fix me up with a firm's car. He also said that his uncle could sometimes be a bit difficult.

I duly arrived at Michael's the night before starting, and after a quick breakfast rode with him in his car to the Monday Market at Campsey Ashe for a 7am start. After meeting voiceless Uncle Claude, I was introduced to Mr Scoffin who lived in Woodbridge and was in charge of the books. Then I met the office staff comprising Mary Pratt from Dallinghoo, who had been there a long while, and young Jean Snowling from Framlingham. Michael showed me how to weigh and book in the fat pigs and introduced me to Jock, our besmocked foreman in charge, and also a gentleman from Ipswich who took details for the subsidy payments. There were other drovers in similar rigouts to Jock, all with their hedge-cut ash sticks.

When I had finished booking in the fat pigs I auctioned the sows, which were usually sold to buyers for the ice cream market where their fat was in demand – thus the trade price usually went up in the summer and down in the winter. Again I was nervous but somehow got through it, although I hated it. I had never sold livestock before and I was stepping into a well-established tradition that I knew little about. The buyers all knew that I was a new boy and I was scared that they would lift my leg – this being the local expression for taking one for a ride. I also gave away my lack of local knowledge by asking even seasoned buyers their names. No one tried to do me down, but the

Monday Market Campsey Ashe.

dealer, Cordy Allen, told me afterwards not to point when taking a bid from him. I realise that they did not want to broadcast to all and sundry that they were bidding.

Next I sold the poultry and rabbits, then the dead game, where a lovely old boy called Ernie Garrod was in charge. I had not got a clue as to the values here, but Ernie, who away from the sale yard was a quite famous judge of our fur and feathered friends, had the values on every lot ready marked in the sale book for me. Claude Spear had already told me that the poultry dealers were as sharp as a bag of chisels and as artful as a wagon load of monkeys.

One week we had 400 hares entered, which was many, many times the usual number. There had been a hare shoot at Sudbourne where there always seemed to be a lot of hares, and we knew that the dealers would be reluctant to bid against one another. So Claude decided to get Ernie to buy the first one in as if he was buying for a private person which would give us a guide as to how much the dealers would go up to for the rest. Ernie duly bought the first hare and then, during the sale, quietly took it round the back of the pens to re-enter it at the end of the sale, so that the dealers would not know. Ernie bought the first hare at four shillings and I proceeded running the dealers up to about three shillings and sixpence for the rest, but when we came to the last one, being the one that Ernie had bought in at four shillings, they cried "A shilling, sir. This one smells." You cannot catch old birds with chaff!

Next, if I was quick, I could grab a cup of tea and a roll at the little café run by Audrey for Mrs Runnacles of Wickham Market. Someone in here said to me, "Yer up from the sheeres boy ain't ye?" which I was to learn was a much-used local expression. I then sold the produce and flowers before moving into the shed to sell the furniture and finally, to sell the timber down the meadow. I looked at my watch, it was half past five and I was quite exhausted. I was however far from finished as I then learned that Mr Scoffin, Claude, his wife Bella, Michael and myself were to meet up about half an hour later at

Claude and Bella's house, 109 The Thorofare in Woodbridge, where every account was to be written out by hand and then checked ready for the cheques to be written out and sent off the next morning. At minutes before closing time Claude Spear took us all over to The Cannon public house, opposite to where he lived, and in his infinite generosity bought us each a light ale.

Tuesday morning arrived and Claude Spear told me that he usually attended Ipswich Corn Exchange, where the firm kept a wooden chandlers stand along with about 50 others who were mainly corn dealers. I attended this with Claude and knew no one, although I recognised the name of a Mr Alan Foster-Clarke from somewhere out Horham way, who had a similar stand almost opposite and who, when we got round to talking, told me that he had bought from me at Cambridge a very unusual set of crawler tracks that he had done quite well with, having sold them on the way home. I remembered them and that he was the only bidder – an instance that made me believe how important research was, both in the full description of the lot and particularly who was the most likely buyer. The non-adventure of this particular lot left me feeling empty and that we had let the vendor down. It made me realise the importance of correct cataloguing and responsibility to one's client – the vendor.

Again I was so embarrassed in this place not being able to join in everyone else's hubbub and the fact that I was Norman no-mates, with no one to speak to at all. I was totally embarrassed and I hated every second of it. At the end of the afternoon Claude took me to Limmer and Pipes in Ipswich for a cup of tea. This was very much like Matthews in Cambridge, only the tradition here was for the Corn Exchange people to stand just inside the door and drink tea standing up. It pleased me to meet Mr Leonard Hempson again, the Ipswich auctioneer who had indirectly got me this job.

By Wednesday I was back in the office at Wickham Market and I was allotted a tiny space in what I reckoned was formerly a broom cupboard! I had sufficient room for only a minute desk and chair, but I did have a very pleasant view from the window over the Market Square. Furthermore it was off Michael's room, so it had great advantage in that, as it had no door, I heard everything that Michael said, so I had a good idea what was going on. For instance for the Christmas Sale I phoned some good buyers that I knew from Cambridge and I learned that our client Tom Kidner from Stoven Hall near Southwold was seeking a large Agricultural Estate. I phoned Frank Grain of Grain and Chalk's off my own bat to see if he had anything.

Unless otherwise instructed, on Thursday and Friday I would normally expect to be measuring and drawing, for the purposes of obtaining grants, plans of land drainage or house improvements. It was a time when many villages were now receiving mains drainage and there was a grant for bringing water closets into the house. Drawing these plans was up my street and I soon followed the style of plan drawing of professional architects and the erect and elongated writing on it likewise. In Mr Scoffin's room were piles of very pressing tenant-right valuations to be worked out. I nevertheless felt lacking in knowledge in this department, as at Grain and Chalk Mr Peter had a German secretary called Herr Schoep who attended to all his valuations, and I felt that I had not been as fully instructed in this matter as I should have been. That is to put it mildly for I had not been instructed at all. This proved to be my undoing, for when Michael had gone with his valuation book and figures to agree a farm tenant-right changeover valuation with another valuer, his figures had been ridiculously out of proportion and an examination showed that it was my fault. He further said that he was lucky that he knew the other side's valuer well and that the other valuer had allowed him to correct my mistakes.

Once Norah Spear had arrived back from Canada, I duly joined her at The Beeches in Melton and, as Michael had envisaged, we got on like a house on fire. She knew almost everyone and filled me in on their backgrounds. A client she had met, named Leslie Maddock-Brew – who had the Mettingham Castle estate, which we managed – was arranging, just before Christmas, a small party for his daughter Angie. He had asked Mrs Spear to take along a few suitable young partygoers as Angie did not know too many local people. Norah Spear had asked local farmer's daughter, Tweedy Mann, myself and others to make up a car load. I believe that our host owned a string of garages in London and must have been a man of influence, as in pride of place on the mantelpiece, was a Christmas card from Harold Macmillan, the current prime minister no less.

As a result of meeting Tweedy, she phoned shortly afterwards to say that her father, Jim Mann, our most important client, had a spare seat at his table at the White Lion at Aldeburgh on New Year's Eve and would I care to go with them. The White Lion at New Year's Eve with dinner and dancing to Mrs Punchard's band was, at that time, the most prestigious place to be, so I duly accepted the invitation. It was here that I met Tweedy's sister Susan's friend Marion Keate, who was on holiday from University College Dublin and who I subsequently dated. Tweedy's partner, Owen Jenkins, who was a tall, dark and handsome young man, was determined to introduce me around. He had no transport of his own and after this evening I duly met him every Friday night at the Bell and Steelyard at Woodbridge where he seemed to know about every party that was going on over the weekend, and was determined that we should go – invited or not!

At this dinner dance a loud voice suddenly boomed at me, "Hello young man." At first I did not recognise him as he had not got his cap pulled down over his eyes, but it was a character from the market called Anthony Hurren, a larger-than-life pig farmer, who would laboriously wait at my elbow, constantly asking how many fat pigs I had booked in. He farmed in the same village as a tenant of Lord Alistair Graham, and would wait till the last minute before sending Bertie Wright, the carrier from Snape, to get his pigs. What he was waiting to know was how many pigs had been entered in the sale, because if he thought that there would be more pigs than to satisfy the market, we would get none of his. But if he thought that we might be short in number for the expected trade, then it was all hell let loose at the very last minute to deliver his pigs. He was a pain, but lovable, as he had a philosophy on everything. On seeing that he had a little blood on his face, I mention it, to be told, "It's them fisher boys, you know 'the ones with earrings'." I had quite forgotten that this was Aldeburgh where fishing was still a trade. Famous for its sprats, this was just about the season for catching them. At a time when no workman would be seen dead with an earring, this was the symbol of the fishing trade, for it was said that a pierced ear would improve one's eyesight. The other symbol of their trade was a sweater called a 'ganzie' which was in heavy tight-knitted dark blue wool, long in the body and tight at the neck. Anthony had helped eject these fisher boys when they stormed the place at midnight, and he had got a bloody nose for his trouble.

I had recently joined Melton Young Farmers, which met at the Village Hall, Melton, once a month, which was just opposite where I was living with Mrs Spear at 'The Beeches', a house that was once the home of the Suffolk artist Thomas Churchyard. Melton was probably the strongest Young Farmers in the county and most of them were the offspring of our clients. Coming from Spears, they all seemed to accept me straight away. Having gone from being almost unable to get a date whilst at college, I thought that I had now landed in Shangri-La, for the young farmer girls here were quite beautiful. However, on reflection, I realised that my biggest asset was probably that I now drove Michael's father's cream Ford Consul number WRT 98, with its red interior trim, front bench seat and steering wheel gear change. With all these assets life proceeded in a social whirl with so many 21st parties and balls to attend that I now needed two evening dress shirts to keep up.

The best evening that I remember was Nigel Pusey's 21st party, which was held at Bealings Village Hall. Here one of our gang – I think that it was Mark Wyner – had gone up on the stage in front of the band to sing 'La Mer' – to hear it even now gives me palpitations as it lets me relive the best parts of all my ramblings which was the best period of my life. We all had our dinner jackets on, and then about 11.30 quickly changed into more suitable attire and went to Nacton Shore where a jazz band had been arranged to play for the rest of the night. Nacton Shore is a sandy beach on the banks of the river Orwell and to see the sunrise here really is something unforgettable. Along these banks is Broke Hall, where Admiral Broke had lived. He had captained the battleship Shannon when beating the Chesapeake off Boston Harbour. This was our only victory in the war that lost us the Americas.

At the Young Farmers I became friendly with Tony Hayward from Ashmoor Hall, Campsey Ashe, on whom I was to play a not very gentlemanly trick that got found out, and it deserved to be, I suppose. There was a certain young lady at the Young Farmers that I knew Tony, amongst others, had his eye on. I was unattached and I quietly asked this young lady if she would like to come with me to a dance that was some distance away at Newmarket Young Farmers. We had a great evening and thought nothing about it. A week or two after this, Tony went to a party at a school pal's in Cambridge, during which time his pal said that he had seen a photograph of yours truly in the *Newmarket Journal* and there I was dancing with his would-be sweetheart. Luckily Tony had the greatest of dispositions and did nothing more than laugh. Some long time after this Tony asked me if I would run his young sister back from a dance at Aldeburgh White Lion. She had not left school at the time, but it was the beginning of a long-term romance that we kept as a secret as long as we could. It was a most enjoyable relationship in which I would spend many a weekend at Tony's playing tennis and going to parties. "You're getting your feet well under the table there boy," said Mother.

I felt that I was getting on well at Spears where I had never had such freedom and recognition. Almost everywhere I went I was known as 'Mr Spear's man', something that I had no idea existed for me when I was almost anonymous at Cambridge, but it was really the people and the area that I loved. They were 50 years behind most of the modern changes, but in my book they were 50 times better for it. The characters at the market were unique. Charlie Howlett from Framlingham, who had long sideburns, smoked a broken clay pipe that appeared to be burning his nose, and wore the obligatory neck 'wropper', would drive Barney his mule to the market loaded with probably a pen of weaner pigs on the bottom of the cart, then a crate of fowls, then whatever produce was in season, and flowers on top or even a stick or two of furniture.

There was another horse and trap that arrived also from Framlingham, which belonged to Valerie Pendle. If Charlie's mule Barney met with Valerie Pendle's pony it would take off and Charlie could not control it. It was said that you could hear Charlie's voice, complete with all sorts of swear words, several fields away, and many is the time that his whole charabanc flew, at uncontrollable speed, across the main A12 London to Yarmouth road. Valerie Pendle's Grandfather, Prince Heffer, was never seen at the market without wearing his hossman's three-piece suit. I had only seen this distinctly Suffolk apparel once before. It had a collar that was high to the neck in front, a Van Dyke arch shaped back, horseshoe buttons in threes and all over stitching in threes, fall-front trousers that were tight to the knee, then flared with three rows of stitching around the bottom. Johnnie Stammers and his brothers, who were poultry dealers, also wore jackets like this, as did their father. These suits were all handmade locally and the 'snips' would be cross-legged whilst sitting on a table, sewing. I thought even then, in the late '50s, where else could you go to find retention and championing of the tradition such as this?

Loads of people from local villages such as Blaxhall, Tunstall, Snape and beyond, would come each week with something to sell, then go and spend the proceeds in The Talbot at Campsey Ashe, a well-known traditional local pub where singing and stepdancing would break out. One day Claude Spear said that Boxer Fairweather had been let out of Melton Institution, and I was not to sell him any items totalling more than £10. When the market was over Boxer would get in The Talbot, play his button accordion and then pass the hat round. I once bought a single row melodeon off Boxer for a pound and he played it whilst our yardman, Fred Smith, did a step dance. This was still in the age of self-entertainment, and I loved every bit of it.

On a Sunday night my mates and I would go to any pub that had music. There was always a piano played at Witnesham 'Barley Mow' where Jock, our head pig drover, was always to be imbibing and also very often Carl Giles, the *Daily Express* cartoonist, who had Hill Brow farm and was known to play the piano. At Gosbeck 'Greyhound', as well there was piano accompaniment, and we would sing "It's a lovely night tonight, the moon is shining bright so let's go round the corner and have a bit on the sly" and all its verses that we dare.

There were also singsongs at Campsey Ashe's Buck, Ashbocking's Nelson, Swilland's Half-Moon, Henley's Cross-keys, Kettleborough's Chequers, Tunstall's Green Man and Blaxhall's Ship, although at the latter two I would get ribbed about the price of pigs or something of that nature. We could always find Charlie Howlett at his brother-in-law, Jimmy Finbow's pub, The Hare at Fram but we did not often go so close to home as there was still class distinction, so it was not really our place, and one could sometimes feel uncomfortable as if we were intruding.

Out of our immediate area I had gone into public bars, perhaps with a friend, and heard the buzz of conversation drop right down on our entry. They hated what were called 'furriners' and I loved them for it for they were preserving their distinct identity. It was the author Adrian Bell who opened his first book *Corduroy* with the line that Suffolk was "a county rich in agricultural detail" – well this was it alright, for I had entered a part of my own county where even female cats had a demarking name – 'Betty' as I soon found out. As much as I was enjoying life there was an ogre in the camp that took a lot of getting round.

CHAPTER 4

Uncle Claude to the Fore

Michael had said that his uncle was difficult and he was right. I would receive notes from Claude Spear whilst I was selling that would refer to a particular person, and that if I sold something to them, and they did not pay, he would hold me responsible and I would then have to call upon them later to get the cash, if I could.

For instance, we were instructed to hold a house sale of contents at Dale Hall Farm, Henley Road, Ipswich, for an old friend of Claude's. We had no sooner fixed the date when the announcement came out that Princess Margaret's wedding would take place on that day. After much discussion Michael and I thought that the sale should be postponed but Claude decided against us and went ahead. It was a time when televisions were just getting established and it seemed that almost everyone had bought a TV to see the Royal Wedding. The sale was, as Michael and I had predicted, a complete disaster and I remember the only dealer, Cousins, and his son Ted, having a field day. Claude, in taking bids in one instant, did not realise it but he had taken bids at 17, 18, 19 shillings, then he said one pound when he had been bidding in pounds when the bid should have been £20. It is easily done as I was to find out.

On many Saturday afternoons Spears held household and small-holders' sales on the property. They were usually great fun. The general idea was to sell the smalls (lots that could be handled easily by one porter) through a ground-floor back window after they had been on view inside the house. Then the furniture would be laid out in lot order round the garden. If it rained you would need to get it inside, probably into an outbuilding. We had recently had some items stolen, so I told the porter who would be handing these small lots out through the window, to make sure that he was alone and that the door was closed. Sure enough a 'nice' old boy with a walking stick asked the porter if he could remain seated in this 'smalls' room. The porter carried on, turning his back to him whilst handing the lots to the 'shower' outside the window, and then waited until the bidding was finished before taking the lot back to the 'finder'. About ten minutes later the 'nice' old boy was standing up by the lots and still the porter took no notice. A few minutes later, as the porter turned around a bit quick, he saw the allegedly 'nice' old boy trying to stuff one of the lots in his pocket. It was just as well that the porter did not tell me until the sale was over.

At one time we used to experience one item going missing at every sale and we did so many things to stop it but could not trap the culprit. If I had caught this petty thief I ask myself if I could have forgiven him.

If we had a lot of smalls, the alternative layout method to this was to lay trestle tables out in two rows with a gap in the middle for two porters to find and show the lots. Chairs would then be set out all round the outside, which would all be occupied by ladies – and I tell no lie when I say that nearly all of them would be knitting! How times have changed.

On another occasion we were putting some guinea fowls in a crate to be viewed and sold, when two escaped. We thought that they would not be able to fly but they could, and they did – right to the top of a large elm tree. When we announced that we would sell them in situ at the top of one of these trees, a lady in the crowd shouted out, "Do you deliver?"

There was much saleroom fun in this era, pre the internet and buyer's premiums, but the thing that really killed the saleroom banter was bidding cards. At the dispersement sale of Coppins, the undertakers at Stradbroke, everyone was packed into the joiner's shop where the coffin boards were to be sold in lots of ten. The auctioneer was standing on a lot of these boards spuffling away when an old boy beneath him lit up some of that strong black Ipswich tobacco known as Churchman's Counter Shag. As the smoke drifted into the auctioneer's direction you could see that it was going to get in his lungs, and when it did, he choked fit to die. At this point an old wag shouted out, "While you're a-selling them coffin boards, sir, do you think that you ought to keep one lot back 'cause that looks as though you're gonna need it yerself." Much mirth all round.

But my biggest memory is how almost all seemed to strut their individual identity in suits, such as the ones that I described earlier I had seen Prince Heffer wearing at the market. These suits would be made to measure, probably by the much-applauded local Stradbroke 'snips' named Curtis and Rowe.

Michael Spear seemed very reserved and would always be deep in thought as we drove along in the car. However, he could be quite humorous when away from the business and out on his boat. Michael's father was a keen sailor and had an oceangoing yacht called *Brambling* which Michael took me out in before it was sold. He told me that they had won the Dover to Marstrand international race and when they were sailing home, "I sat on the side of the boat with an empty cigarette packet in one hand, and a very important key to part of the boat in the other. Guess which one I threw overboard?" He said he had not thrown the empty cigarette over as he intended but the important key and they had a rare job to improvise to sail the boat home. I can see him doing it as he was so often not quite in the moment.

On another occasion he told me of a very lucky escape that he had. Michael did a lot of planning applications for new farm buildings and had been asked to arrange for a massive range of new cattle fattening sheds to be erected for the firm's largest client, Jim Mann of Bawdsey. Jim Mann did nothing in a small way. At that time Michael thought that although the building was massive, planning permission was not necessary as it stood more than 40 feet from a road. However, when it was all up and completed the council served notice that they considered that it did require planning permission, and that within 28 days it was to be pulled down. Michael said that the Ipswich solicitor, Tommy Symes, objected on behalf of Jim Mann, and a hearing was arranged at Ipswich. "I walked up the steps to the courtroom with my heart in my shoes," said Michael. "I had just lost my father and now had let down, extremely badly, our biggest friend and client." Tommy Symes, said Michael, "replied to their opening salvo that they had served their notice under such and such law and this law stated that another demand should have been issued. It was quickly established that this council notice had not been served and that we were free to walk. What a let off!"

It is never all over until the fat lady sings.

Spears managed the Mettingham Castle estate, where I had been to the party that I described earlier, for Leslie Maddock-Brew. To get there you had to go through Halesworth, and it was here that I discovered a little corner café where I got an excellent three-course luncheon for two shillings and sixpence. I told Michael and he had apparently been there just the same. It was excellent value and shows how prices have changed. It was however not as inexpensive as the similar one that I used to go to when I was with Grain and Chalk. This was run by a fellow who we called Bill on behalf of Bull's Dairy. It was situated about a quarter of a mile down the Cherry Hinton Road, in Cambridge, and a three-course lunch there cost just two shillings. How did he do it? Well I suppose that it was only ten years after the war. The old country was bereft and had to have loans from the USA. Rationing had only just finished and there was still a general air of frugality. It was somehow part of a game to save. I used to see Bill buying produce at the market from the firm of Robert Bell, whose auctioneer, John Riddy, would sell lots and take the cash at the same time. Later on he was to work for Grain and Chalk, who over the years having amalgamated with Cheffins of Saffron Walden, took their name.

Spears market was on a Monday as was Cambridge and that is the best day as most meat is sold for the weekends and butchers can get out from the shop on a Monday. "There was a ring in Halesworth market before the war which virtually killed it," explained Michael. "This meant that we could now draw cattle from beyond Halesworth, in fact right up to Kessingland near Lowestoft. Arthur Bloss the big cattle dealer from Melton was a good friend," he said, "and I would phone him on a Sunday night to ask how the trade had been on the previous Saturday at Norwich, which he always attended. If Arthur said that the trade was likely to be good, I had a host of farmers where I could draw cattle, such as the Flemings from Eyke, Edwards from Rishangles Lodge and Arthur Mortier of Hollesley, who always had good white-faced Herefords, and they all appreciated being approached to be told that the trade should be good." During the period that I was at Spears, Michael had raised the average number of fat beasts sold each week from 40 to 100.

I had worked hardly at all for my 1960 final exam and as antic-ipated I had failed. I had not bothered too much as my exemption was keeping me out of the National Service which was due to finish about then. I did not want to be the last to get the call-up, so took things lightly. However, I knew that I had to pass the exam in 1961 if I could, but I was having such a good time that studying by home correspondence course was nigh impossible. I had been impressed with the College of Estate Management when I had passed the inter-mediate exam and remembered how the final term had been set to revision alone. I enquired of the college if it was possible to pay and join them for their final spring term, immediately prior to the examination and found that it was. I approached Michael and said, "If I attend the Cattle Market on a Monday over the next two months or so, and worked on the Tuesday, and guaranteed to keep up to date with the land drainage plans, could I have the rest of the week off at no pay?" Michael discussed it with Claude and apparently had some difficulty in getting him to agree, but when he came back to me he said "Yes" reluctantly, so I duly found out about staying at the most convenient London YMCA.

I furthermore disciplined myself to not going out until the exam was over. Having enjoyed Christmas, I then got my head down. I knew that it was the only way that I could do it. Girls would be out of the question. I nevertheless made the young lady that I was friendly with my last thought at bedtime and the first the following morning and I believe that having something to look forward to drove me on. It seemed to work and as exhausted as I got with doing my studies at home or drainage plans on a Saturday and Sunday morning even, I managed to pass. I remember the morning at the office, when the letter arrived telling me of my success – everyone seemed delighted for me and Michael said that I had hoodwinked the examiner, whatever that may mean. I duly phoned mates Tony Hayward, Ian King and Martin Greenfield and we went on a pub crawl in Framlingham, where there was a 'devil among the tailors board' and made up a rule that anyone knocking all nine pegs down with one throw would have to buy a round. There were quite a few nines-in-one throws. We then went back to Martin's in Marlesford for coffee and tried not to appear over tipsy when his Mother joined us. It was a magnificent way of getting all those academic chores off my chest, and Spears were to put up my salary from £675 per annum to £750, which caused me to think that I now had my feet well under the table, but nothing stays the same!

I BID YOU FAREWELL

One Sunday evening towards the end of the year I had gone for a drink with a mate down to the picturesque Ramsholt Arms on the Bawdsey peninsula. I knew this area well, as almost as soon as I arrived at Spears they had sold the Quilter estate in Bawdsey including the historic Ramsholt Arms in conjunction with Jackson-Stops. I remember this quite well because at the pre-sale auction, when the small-tenanted properties were sold off, Jackson-Stops' auctioneer started off at one, two, three, four, five etc., at which the potential buyer shouted out, for he thought that he was bidding in hundreds whilst the auctioneer was taking his bids in thousands. Another lesson learned – make the price plain as well as who is bidding and for what lot!

It was always pleasant at the Ramsholt Arms, and at the end of the evening I followed Robert Shepherd in his Triumph sportscar along the long private road that led to the main road. Robert put his foot down and so did I. The only difference was that Robert's car slowed at the junction and mine did not. Hitting a load of wet leaves, the car skidded into the bank, and I was to be told that it was a write-off.

Mother had given Uncle Joe £10 for his old Hillman Minx at this time, and it stood in her yard. I asked if I could borrow it until my replacement car arrived. I was feeling down but unbeknown to me things were about to get better.

"Hello, who is that?" I said on answering the telephone at Mother's where I had gone to stay for the weekend. "It's John Boardman," came the reply, "and it is Neil Lanham that I would like to speak to." I knew that he was a chartered surveyor from Haverhill as I had heard him speak at the dinner and annual meeting of the Suffolk Branch of the Central Association of Agricultural Valuers. He said, "I was wondering if you would be interested in a position here in Haverhill. I am aware that you have recently passed your exam and I wondered if it would interest you?" It is extraordinary that he should phone at this time as I was feeling a bit miffed about losing my status by having to drive what in my eyes was a cheap and lowly replacement Ford car, which was about the only crack in my armour so to speak. I was, nevertheless, as happy as a sandboy with my life at Wickham Market. But one should never look a gift horse in the mouth, so I pretended to be enthusiastic and agreed to go and meet him. I had no intention of taking the position, but I was nosey. I was exceedingly happy in my job, had my girlfriend whose friendly parents I went to stay most weekends, also a close set of Young Farmer friends and the cattle market which I loved.

It was on a very wet November evening that I took the road for Haverhill. As the leaves fell across the rainswept road and clustered in my windscreen, I listened to a story on the car radio about a famous lawyer who had risen to the top from most modest means, and how he had sheltered from the storm in a doorway to be taken in by a family. This had led to him being involved, in a very minor way, in a lengthy lawsuit on their behalf and he had seized the moment to change the case. In my romantic mind, I paralleled myself with the great man, for here was I, in 1961, proceeding to go for an interview with Mr John T Boardman, Auctioneer of Haverhill. It seemed to my mind that my younger years had prepared me for this moment. Nevertheless, I was never going to take this job – I was so happy in my life in East Suffolk.

Before I arrived at Spears I had been used to driving prewar bangers, all of which had broken down regularly. I had to learn to push, fiddle with the carburettor or with the sparks in order to get my transport in motion, so on the face of it whatever offer that may be coming forward appeared to put me back to that again.

I arrived at Burton Cottage in Haverhill, where John Boardman lived, about 7.30 in the evening having made the journey over in my Mother's old Hillman Minx, which I had borrowed. I knocked on the door and, on its opening, said "Hello" to a fresh-faced young lady who explained that she was Anna, Mr Boardman's daughter. She was about my own age and her presence I found quite cheering. Mr Boardman arrived in plus fours and bald head, and told me that he had been conducting an auction sale that day of timber, and I guessed that he had been dressed in his tweed plus fours to be the part. He, I was to discover later, would always be dressed for the part. Black bowler to open the Trustee Savings Bank in Haverhill, and the grey bowler would come out for the South Suffolk Agricultural Association show – he was treasurer, following in his father's shoes, showing a continuity of about 50 years. I had been told, in this era when no one was seen in shorts, John Boardman would wear his, even to the office. He was his own man and likeable, and as a hangover from the Victorian era, he was not bound by all of the modern conventions. He had not joined the Masons, and at a Rotary dinner, I had been told, when the Masonic members had been standing up and toasting one another across the room he had stood up and said, "The vicar wishes to take wine with all his parishioners." This little stand against authority appealed to me as I too was a bit of a rebel.

So we left Burton Cottage to walk out of his back gate and across the Downs, to show me the office. As we walked, he told me that the Downs was a new estate of houses they were selling for the Crossman Development Company with semi-detached houses at £2,550 each. It seemed that John Boardman and his family had owned the Downs and thus they had reserved the right to be involved in the sale of the houses. Nevertheless another firm of estate agents had moved into the town and their red and black boards were everywhere. They had already been given this estate to sell. Haverhill, it seemed, had stood still and, being 18 miles from anywhere, had stagnated.

We crossed the road and arrived at the office. Now auctioneers' offices are known for being old-fashioned and preserving of their traditional ways, but this office was a step back to Victorian history. It stood on a prominent corner in the town, at the junction of the Cambridge Road, the Bury St Edmunds Road and the new relief road, which had been put in recently to stop the main Colchester traffic from going through this town centre. The office had double front doors for some reason, and the main window onto the street, along the Pightle side, had been completely boarded up many years before, probably during the last century. It hadn't had a lick of paint for a similar time.

The boarded floor of the front office was well-worn across to the clerks' door on the far corner beneath its linoleum covering. A single twisted electric flex hung from the ceiling, down to a circular Aladdin's-hat-shaped shade that had been pulled by a piece of binder twine, so that it lit up the typewriter on the small desk of the 18-year-old typist, who had been fairly recently recruited to sit there. There were plans and old notices stuffed everywhere, and a big bench along the side did nothing, and had not been touched – apart from to drag out the old set of lot numbers – for years.

In the back room, where the clerk sat, was a window looking out over a yard with odd auctioneers' equipment dumped in it as well as leftover lots from sales, presumably that the shilling bidder had failed to collect. There was a coal fire in an office that lay beyond the front reception room, then in a recess to one side was the safe where the clerk, 78-year-old Jack Webb, kept the leatherbound ledgers which he would take out each morning. These were each about 2′6″ by 2′ and seemingly weighed about half a hundredweight each. To the right-hand side of the fireplace was the filing system – pigeon-holes and, by now, the decaying atmosphere almost made me expect to see pigeons nesting in them. These pigeonholes lined up about five across the top by about eight deep, which would give enough to cover the alphabet, and correspondence for each client was put into reused manila envelopes.

The Belgian cotton carpet, presumably another lot left over from a sale, was worn, tattered and faded to grey scale. The door to the left hand of the central office was to John Boardman's room. The

Georgian mahogany bookcase to the right held copies of Woodfall's, Landlord and Tenant, etc., and the Agricultural Holdings Act, and a special timber measuring tape called 'hoppus's foot'. It also held Mr Boardman's stack iron in a leather case which was used for assembling to thrust deep into a haystack to pull out a sample to test its quality. There were also brass-mounted sectional rods for dipping ale barrels, and an old print of Haverhill hung on the wall. The lino floor covering shone in the centre but not in the dusty corners, and across the room was a side table which supported the stick telephone – displaying the number Haverhill 6. This, apparently, was the deluxe model, for whilst one spoke down a rosette on the top of a stick, one could use not just the single earpiece for one's left ear, but a further one for the right ear as well.

The window on the station side housed an ill-lit and faded plan of the Downs estate, posters of a forthcoming farm sale, and contractor equipment for the executors of a Steeple Bumpstead gentleman who had died recently.

Despite all the dead flies that had accumulated along the bottom of the windowsills, I found that the timeless nature seemed to be pregnant with umpteen hidden stories yet to be revealed, which in a quirky sort of way appealed to this lover of eccentricity.

We returned to Burton Cottage, where Mr Boardman told me he was prepared to offer me a salary of £1,000.00 per annum. My present one was £750.00 and had been increased from £675.00 upon my passing my final of the Chartered Auctioneers exams. I hadn't had much money before, so this seemed good to me. I would have to buy a car, but Mother had said that I could borrow £200 from her to add to the £200 that I had already saved which was sufficient to acquire a year-old Morris Minor. Anyway, this would be better than that dreadful Anglia that I was about to be demoted by. Still, I was only coming to have a look round; I wasn't taking this job was I? Or was I? But here, I would have a newfound status of assistant. I told him I would have a think about it and let him know within a short while. We then went through to officially be introduced to Anna, his daughter, and Mrs Boardman, Molly. Molly was the daughter of a local publican and Charles Boardman, John's father, had apparently not approved of this association, which was much the same as Michael Spear and his wife Margaret, who had worked under her Mother at the Campsey Ashe Market tearoom.

Burton Cottage was a big prestigious house in the centre of the town, with gardens. It had belonged to an auntie of John's, from whom he had acquired it. The large garden included a grass tennis court upon which Mr Boardman would strut in his white shorts on Sunday afternoons, entertaining the local social tennis elite. He kept a gardener, Tom Morgan, who was also head porter at the sales and put up the sale boards that, if the truth be told, had appeared increasingly infrequently. Tom had been a horse-riding instructor in the 1914–18 war and would tell us of how he had instructed the winning rider in the Grand National. Apparently, from time to time, he had days without speaking to Mr Boardman, but I never saw him in this light. There always seems to be a strange relationship between employer and gardener. Just whose garden is it I wonder? It is the guvnor's but it is the gardener's as well so there is bound to be conflict?

After the exchange of pleasantries and a small alcoholic refreshment, I pondered the realities of moving from the area that I loved, where people had been good and kind to me, and where I seemed to have found a footing in life that had previously eluded me.

After I thought about it for a few days, I told Michel Spear that I had been offered another job with a view to a partnership and asked if there was any hope of a partnership in the future if I stayed on at Spear's. To this he gruffly replied, "You've a lot to learn," and said nothing more. Again I thought for a few days and came to the conclusion that maybe he was right. I did have a lot to learn but it would not happen here. I had been so enthusiastic in building up clients when drawing plans for the land drainage grant, and when I went on site I would ask all the drivers on the drain-laying machines where they were going next, and ask them to put in a good word for us. These plans now took up over half the week. I could see myself getting stuck as the drainage plans dogsbody in the same way as I had been the sale plans dogsbody at Cambridge. So with a very heavy heart I told Michael that I was going, and gave in my notice to have effect from the end of the year. If Michael had said one word of encouragement I would not have been able to bring myself to depart, but I suppose that his problem was his difficult uncle. I had now made my bed so I had to lie on it. However a new world of opportunity awaited me and I thought that I was ready to embrace it, come what may.

CHAPTER 5

The New World Order

K nowing that Mr Boardman was shorthanded, and that he had a farm dispersal sale in December at Durrant's, a large agricultural contractor's business in Steeple Bumpstead, I asked that I should have a day off from Spears and attend. He approved. Afterwards he said that he had good comments and referring to the noise that I had made someone had even said, "The rooks won't sleep about there tonight."

It was an absolutely bitter cold day with snow thick upon the ground. In those days the local policeman would attend all outside auction sales but on this day he could not, so asked the copper from Radwinter to attend on his behalf. There was an alcohol bar at this sale, and when the Bumpstead copper found that he could attend after all. Someone asked him in out of the cold, and he was just putting a whiskey to his lips when his mate from Radwinter appeared and, having cycled over in this raw bitterly cold weather, was frozen stiff. Amidst many old Bumpstead smiles he turned the air as blue as his white with frost uniform now was.

On the 2nd of January 1962, I arrived at Boardman's office. It was late afternoon and Margaret, the young lady in the front office, welcomed me. I should have arrived the day before, but it had been a terrible winter and it had been impossible to get through from Campsey Ash where I had spent the New Year. Margaret, the firm's typist/secretary, straightaway offered to get me some tea. Jack Webb the clerk instantly came through. I had not been introduced to Jack Webb before. He quickly said that we had better walk round to Mrs Argent's where we had arranged for me to have some lodgings at 33 Chauntry Road, which I found was one of a terrace, there being many terraced houses in Haverhill. I was to find that this was because of the weaving industry. This one was slightly better as it had a garden in the front as well as a garden at the back. Mrs Argent was sharp and to the point. It seemed she hadn't wanted a lodger but had been talked into it, and she laid down the rules to me very firmly. She was a goodly soul, but I realised that I had to mind my 'P's and 'Q's or I would be out. Anyway, I settled in at Chauntry Road and turned up at 2 Station Road at nine o'clock the following morning.

"Cup of tea Mr Lanham?" said Jack Webb as I arrived. "Thank you very much indeed," I replied. He showed me to my appointed office upstairs, but I quickly realised that this was never ever going to work, and all my experiences of the lonely Cambridge garret came flooding back. I asked "Is there any possible way that I could sit downstairs?" – which meant being in a corner of his office. He reluctantly agreed and arranged for a small card table for me to work at.

Jack Webb was 78. He had gone to the Cangle School on the opposite corner to the office and had to pay one penny a week, tradesman's sons were tuppence. He was a mine of information and would take off his sock without the slightest hesitation to show us his hammer toe he got playing football.

The history of the firm of Chas. Boardman & Son is interesting. In 1895, a young Charles Boardman, a qualified auctioneer, had arrived from Spellmans of Norwich. He took over the Haverhill firm of Fitch and Goodchild who in turn had taken over from others going back to 1824. He married a Miss Gurteen, from the wealthy local family of clothing manufacturers of that name, and who also owned a great deal of local farmland. He was on about every committee, including the Suffolk Agricultural Association, and was a captain in the local part-time Territorial Army. He was popular, and considerably expanded the firm in all directions. He lived at Abbotts Hall, Sturmer, and had several children, including a son John, who followed him into his business as a chartered auctioneer and estate agent. One of his sisters had married Merrick Griffiths, the auctioneer at Newmarket. He had gone to the war to fight for his country and John Boardman had kept an eye on his business whilst he was away, hence Boardmans had several farmers' annual agricultural valuations in the Newmarket area, including Lord Derby's stud, and others as far away as Isleham in Cambridgeshire.

After the war Merrick had recommended his brother-in-law John as the horse auctioneer for selling races at courses such as Huntingdon and Towcester. I always thought that Merrick was a bit of an old stuffed-shirt until I learned that when younger he had played in a dance band, as I used to in a country dance band, and found great fun at it without being too professional. We became quite friendly after that, and I sold several paintings for him when he retired. In his will he left me an interesting allegorical primitive oil painting of Yarmouth Roads with a horserace in the foreground, and Nelson's Column and his warship *Victory* at anchor. I still have it as it reminds me that not only was Nelson a good old Norfolk boy but his passion for his beloved lady was such that after his victory in the Battle of the Nile, the first person that he wanted to share his victory with was Emma, his lady love, apparently then resident at Great Yarmouth.

Adrian Bell – who in 1920 came as a farm pupil to Great Lodge Farm, Hundon, which was about six miles away – attended Haverhill Market, where he practised his trade and referred to Charles Boardman as "the auctioneer with the buttonhole" in his bestselling book *Corduroy*. Charles Boardman's son John, like his father, was never seen without a floral buttonhole.

Charles and his son John Boardman.

I BID YOU FAREWELL

The firm was very strong then but appeared to become complacent in the years following the 1939–45 war. John Boardman, like his father, enjoyed his social life and I knew that he had suffered from leukaemia for some time, and was told he had to have his blood changed every month, which caused him to take the following day off from work.

The cattle market had been closed for a few years before I arrived, and everything oozed decay. It was an opportunity, but as I settled in I wondered if it had gone too far? Michael Spear's words echoed in my head: "You've got a lot to learn" and I knew it, for this country firm had been used to doing many things – in fact everything to do with land and buildings that a small market town might require. I had not even thought about, let alone trained in, such things as public houses, or dealt in all manner of changeover valuations, many of which had a set procedure of their own. Then there were valuations of standing timber, full live and deadstock farm valuations, and unexhausted manurial values. The sale of every type of freehold property by private treaty and auction was something that I had watched but never attempted myself. Likewise lettings, structural surveys and many other things. In most respects it was difficult to not feel like a greenhorn, whose pretence was waiting to be blown!

The day after arriving at Boardmans, I attended the funeral of my very dear friend Mike Newman who was a partner with his father in the corn and seed firm J L Newman & Son of Swaffham Bulbeck. He was only about 22 years old and had everything going for him. He was all that I was not – tall, dark, well-connected and handsome; he'd had a public school education at Greshams and played both hockey and rugby for Cambridge clubs, as well as being chairman of local organisations. He had gone into hospital for a simple hernia operation that had gone wrong. I paid my respects to Shirley, his widow. It was, and still is, as I think of him, a defining moment in my life, bringing home how precious life is and to make the most of it.

The day following this we held an auction dispersal sale of surplus sugar beet equipment, due to a change in farming policy, for Keith Roberts at Hall Farm, Little Wratting. He was the firm's biggest client, much as Jim Mann had been at Spears. He was chairman of the Clare Rural District Council and later became chairman of the National Farmers Union for the country. Above all he was a stalwart friend to Boardmans, at a time when many others were leaving the sinking ship. His wife Ann, and secretary Janet Tucker, put on great refreshments for us, and he continually gave big encouragement to the two auctioneers. Keith Roberts was as solid as they come, and I felt that he approved of John Boardman's new man as he kept saying, "Well done the auctioneers." Whenever I went up to do his Annual Valuation for income tax I was always asked to stay for lunch and he would invariably ask someone else as well, such as Teddy Burgon, the irascible old retired local veterinary surgeon, who had oodles of amusing stories about his life as a vet to a camel platoon in the First World War.

Then next day when Mr Boardman was out, Margaret, the secretary, said, "Will you take this urgent note over to Pauline Edge, who is secretary to William Blake, the Clerk of the Haverhill Urban District Council?" This I duly did and awaited the reply. Unbeknown to me, Margaret was an old friend of Pauline's and the note read "This is our new assistant, what do you think of him?" It was the first of many pranks that I was to have played on me by the firm's mischievous secretary. On another occasion, having been told that some big developers were coming down from London, she had gone out the back, into the primitive conditions of the toilet, and hung a printed sign on the door reading 'To Let' only she had wittingly inserted an 'i' in the middle. Margaret also knew that having admired the singing in the public houses in East Suffolk I was looking for any local people who might carry these old traditional folksongs. A handwritten letter duly arrived at the office with details of all sorts of interesting songs. I had been completely taken in yet again.

John Boardman said, "The Farmers Ball is coming up, Neil, at Haverhill Town Hall, and I think that it would be a good opportunity for us to go and introduce you to a few clients. Have you got a partner? If so I will get four tickets for us." He then said, "The older people play whist first, so I think that you and I should go to that, then come back for the ladies for the dancing. You do play whist don't you?" When I told him that I had not played for some time he said, "I think that we should have a practice first." When we got round to this game at their house I found that it was them who needed the practice, and that they were more likely to trump their partner's ace than I was. It was a great old-time occasion that could well have graced Adrian Bell's book *Corduroy*.

Master John, as Jack Webb called him, had not been too well, and when instructions came from the Suffolk County Council to inspect and value, for sale purposes, the goods of a deceased intestate gentleman who had lived in a council house at 2 School Road, Kedington, I replied that we could hold a little auction at his house. This we did on 18th April 1962, starting at 5.30pm. A single, double-sided, foolscap duplicated sheet formed the catalogue. Smalls were shown out of the back ground-floor window, with furniture around the garden. My friend Paul Gooderham, the auctioneer from Cheffins, came over with his wife Stella, and we all ended up down the pub by 9pm. It was a great natural occasion that could not happen now.

One day Mrs Argent said that she could no longer take me as a lodger on account of the illness of a close relative; I then took lodgings with a young couple who had one daughter. They did not get in until about 5.30pm of an evening, and this was in the midst of one of the worst winters on record. In fact we had been skating for several weeks along the college backs on the River Cam. Their modern house on the Downs estate in Haverhill had no central heating so I used to go over to the Rose and Crown until I thought that they would have lit the fire, and then I went back in time for my usual beans on toast. I did not have a proper bed but a put-you-up and woke up many times in the night as the blanket only tucked in one side, because this long and narrow thing was not intended for sleeping. There was ice on the inside of the window every morning, but strangely enough I did not get a cold all winter.

When the husband's outfitter's job folded, I then moved in with a Mrs N. Brown-Thake, who had a reputation for being a fierce old-time landlady. "Your breakfast will be fried and put on the table at eight o'clock," she said. "At three minutes past, I shall put it under the grill and at five minutes past, the gas will be turned off." The evening dinner was regimented much the same. My plate was always swimming in gravy, and when she delivered it, she carried the plate in a manner that her thumb was invariably in my gravy. I knew that one complaint and I would be out, so my ploy was to get even by leaving a big heap of mustard on the side of the now empty plate so that she could see it, then on handing her my plate, I would give it a sharp short swing to one side at the very last minute so that her thumb landed in the mustard. One-nil to the Arsenal.

I left Brownie when she said that she was going on holiday and demanded lodging money from me just the same. Thinking that this was very unfair, I went with a Mr and Mrs Williams, who had two sons still at school. With them I was more than happy for the rest of my lodging days.

Jack Webb, also known as 'Secy' as he had been secretary of just about everything in the town, was a throwback to a bygone age. He really was a mine of information on auctioneering over the previous half century and more. He had been born in 1885 and would brandish the page in Mr Charles Boardman's diary for 1897 which read "office boy Webb starts." He was 12 then and had been paid two shillings and three pence a week, which was raised by three pence when he went to learn shorthand. Mr Boardman had then bought him a Remington typewriter which was the first one in Haverhill.

I BID YOU FAREWELL

He had been with the firm for 65 years and the whole place told the tale of it. His stories however were what made him unique, as he carried stories around auctioneering that went further back than anyone I could remember. They all had a principle of understanding that could be carried forward. He spoke of the very bad winter of 1895 and how Gurteens had opened a soup kitchen at the clothing factory, and one of their farms had thrashed out peas and oats that were sold to the poor people at a penny a quarter. Furthermore, his father had taught him how to trap sparrows for sparrow pie. About this time a cow at the auction would make around £5. He said that at an auction a cattle dealer from Horseheath named Bill Scott had tried to bid for a poor old cow but could not catch Mr Boardman's eye. At last he shouted out, "Can I bid, Mr Boardman?" "Why of course you can, Bill" came the reply, to which he retorted, "Then I bid you farewell," which I have made the title of this book.

There had been an unknown man, from away, who came to the auction and had bought and taken away, a bunch of store cattle without paying. Mr Boardman guessed that they would turn up again somewhere nearby, so he sent Jack on a journey around all the local markets, starting at Cambridge market which was held on the Monday, Saffron Walden on Tuesday, Bury St Edmunds on Wednesday – until he found them. Then he spoke to the auctioneer who duly cooperated in getting the money back.

Jack would walk anywhere it seemed, and had stories of cycling to Cambridge, then putting his bike on the train "because it was such a lovely night that I wanted to walk back with my mates". It seemed that people were quite prepared to walk almost anywhere in Jack's era, and I remember him walking the four miles to Steeple Bumpstead and the four miles back, just for a fairly inconsequential piece of information in a valuation. One of his favourite things was, in the autumn, to take the keys of all the unoccupied houses that we had for sale to collect for himself the fruit from the gardens. He was a crafty old soul alright. It was when Jack talked about the days that he was secretary of the Haverhill Gala that his eyes lit up, for apparently this was really something, and like Chas Boardman's sheep sales, people came for miles. There were bicycle races organised by Haverhill Wheelers, fancy dress, a beauty queen show, the Co-op brass band, a fair, and it apparently terminated in a torchlight procession. Jack Webb seemed to be involved in everything.

Mr Webb's office was the back room off the central front office, with the door left permanently open, so he could see everyone who came in through the front door. He generally worked at two massive leather-bound ledgers in which he was constantly writing. He would continually have a cigarette drooping from his lips which would have about half an inch of ash hanging, which would then fall onto his handwritten ledger and have to be brushed off. If he was not smoking he would be rattling his favourite sweets, sherbet lemons, around his ill-fitting false teeth. Margaret Sadler seemed to revel in Jack Webb's eccentricities, and loved repeating these tales, taking the part of all the performers.

At the age of 15, Jack had helped at the cattle market which was then held behind the Haverhill Corn Exchange, and in July of that year he helped with the sheep sales which were then 10,000 head and more. On the Sunday before the Bank Holiday Monday, specially laid on trains from Sudbury would bring in as many as 2,000 lambs. These lamb sales were held in a seven-acre field along Wratting Road, and when Mr Boardman inspected preparations he found that many of the men were imbibing down at The Prince of Wales. He then had a hogshead of beer (36 pints) sent up at his expense, to keep them on site. These sheep sales were such an important event that children were allowed time off from school to help. Jack was secretary for the well-known Haverhill Gala from 1911, and after the 1914–18 war to 1939. He also helped raise £1,000 towards a Spitfire aeroplane in the 1939–45 war. He was secretary of Haverhill Rovers football team from 1905–11 and when they played away on the Essex side, for ten shillings extra he would get the train to come on to Haverhill instead of stopping at the Great Yeldham depot.

The Weavers Arms, at the top of Hamlet Road, was known as 'The Pad and Can' and was a well-known call for tramps who paid four pence for their night's lodgings – the tramps being on a weekly tour which took them from The Walnut Tree in Sudbury to Haverhill, Linton, Newmarket, Bury St Edmunds and back to Haverhill. At four pence in Haverhill, they apparently had a proper bed to lay on, as at many places they only had what was known as a 'penny lean upon' and had to stand up all night with a wall to lean against. Footballers from Sudbury who were paid one shilling and four pence would sometimes walk over the night before the match and stay at 'The Pad and Can', saving a shilling. He said that the first football team in Haverhill was called The River and Globe, and they used to play along the bottom of Crowland Road in Haverhill with a ball made of worsted wool. The name of Camping Close along the Pightle however comes from a pre-rules football game that is only found in Suffolk, Norfolk and part of Cambridgeshire and goes back to medieval England.

In Steeple Bumpstead, camping land is still used for both football and cricket. Hanger's Hill was the place where people were hung, and it is situated near Haverhill Hall. The two market fairs in Haverhill were held at Lady Day and Michaelmas as are the usual farm tenant-right changeover dates. Suffolk and Norfolk are different from most other counties, and used the old Gregorian dates of 12th May and 11th October. We simply did not alter our calendar like the modern people 'up in the sheers'. Jack said that the Cattle Market was originally held along the High Street and there was deemed to be a free market at Peas Hill for the poor people. In the Domesday Book apparently it states that the Tihel de Helion, who came over from Normandy with William the Conqueror, was the first lord of the manor of Haverhill and received a third of all market profits. Apparently he had built a timber castle for himself at Helions Bumpstead.

Jack told about auction sales during the tithe wars when the farmers in the 1920s had rejected the right of the church to charge them with an annual payment for… just being farmers. He spoke of tractors being sold at auction for 11 shillings and then the proceeds being given back to the farmers who had clubbed together in determination, and how a certain church bell would be rung when the farmers got wind of the coming of the bailiff's enforcers. Jack Webb even carried folklore such as when he told us that "Winter was not over until we had a Camps snow" – meaning that the final snow of the year in Haverhill will always come from the direction of Castle Camps. He also told of the old witch that had lived off the Withersfield Road and that her name was Anne Suckling, and also of a well-known antique dealer called Hubby Webb who had a cottage along Camps road. Apparently Webb had an immense knowledge but won fame only for murdering his wife.

One of Jack's favourite sayings was "Winter draws on." Then after a long pause he would add "Have you got yours on?" Or in spring after a heavy rainfall he would say, "This will spoil the little potatoes" meaning that it will make them into big ones. Jack had experienced a long history of the toing's and froing's and almost all that was good or could go wrong in the oeuvre of the auction.

The contentment in poverty of the ordinary people impressed me and I lapped up the wisdoms in his stories of valuable experience. However, whilst he had not moved with the times in auctioning he had experienced the ways of people and what they would do in certain circumstances which I had not. I found that many people were too quick to write him off as a silly old fool, but whilst I had not gained much physically it all stood me in good stead for what was to come.

I quickly made a few friends, mainly through the Young Farmers in Haverhill, but it was not like the life I had led in East Suffolk, and more than anything I missed the cut and thrust of the market. The characters were different and seemed not so hail-fellow-well-met. I saw a job advertised in Bedford Market and applied for it. They had big Saturday livestock sales. I got an interview but was not there at the final whistle. I looked at other jobs listed and thought of Rhodesia even, where my classmate Mick Leach had told me in his letters that he liked his job in the Bulawayo police force.

I was drawing plans of cottage conversions and drew a shop modernisation for a builder in Saxmundham by the name of Gissing. Mr Gissing was a lovely old boy as is typically found in East Suffolk, who could do the work as well as anyone – probably better, but like many could not cope with the "damned learned scientific stuff". I had no training in this but thought if others can do it, why cannot I? I would do these plans in my bedroom of an evening and take them to him at the weekend.

I would get copies done at the Haverhill Architects Office of Joe Myers. Joe worked alone and on seeing my plans he asked could I do some surveys and plans for him, which, with Mr Boardman's approval, I did through the firm. One day Joe came to me asking, "Could you do some levels for me for a factory extension?" to which I replied, "Yes, I will have a go" not realising that it was for a massive extension of the factory belonging to International Flavours and Fragrances, one of the biggest new factories in the town. Joe knew that Board-mans kept a theodolite and although I had not done anything like it before I drew a scale drawing of the field, then drew lines across it in scale, which formed squares where I could take a reading at each place the lines crossed. I then went to the labour exchange where I picked up a boy who cost me a pound for the day. On my plan I then marked a datum line which would run an imaginary accurate level plain all over the plot, so that I could then take measurements down from this, using the theodolite.

Joe came up to see how we were getting on and approved. I asked how much I should charge, and we agreed a fee for the day of £10 with £1 for the boy. I enjoyed the work as I had accomplished something

THANK YOU ERIC, BUT WOULD YOU **PLEASE** MOVE TO ONE SIDE

new, and it was mind over matter. Looking back I wonder how on earth I dare take on such a highly skilled and responsible job. I had no training at all. It was simply that I had little to do and a job lay before me, and I fearlessly took the opportunity. What if I had got it wrong? There was no such thing as professional indemnity insurance in those days and if there had been I am sure that Boardmans would not have paid for it. I have often wondered since if the builders that followed this cursed idiot who took erroneous levels was responsible for a wonky flavour-making laboratory, but no one has come yet!

Back at the office I was not a happy bunny. I did a household inventory check on a vacating residential tenancy, only for the owner to complain to Mr Boardman that I had not checked it properly. The tenant had burnt a hole in a cushion and concealed it by putting the cushion the wrong way up and I had not noticed it. There was another complaint about me when I measured out a building plot of land for one dwelling. It was tight and the buyer complained to Mr Boardman that I had not allowed him enough land. The gentlemanly Mr Boardman never said a word. By tradition Boardmans always did the changeover valuation on certain pubs in the area. On hearing that Greene King had appointed another valuer, Mr Boardman had phoned Greene King, which had confirmed that this was the case. I quietly listened to Mr John, thinking that our client was the outgoing landlord, not Greene King and that I would have phoned him and asked him why, as it was up to him, the outgoer, to appoint who he liked, and not Greene King. Losing clients like this got to me, but I was the new kid on the block and had no clout.

I regretted at this time leaving Spears and the cattle market, and I even sent to the Australian Embassy for emigration papers. You could get assisted passage then and I wondered about it. I had read books by the incomparable Australian national poet Banjo Patterson – his stories of the bush were very much like the ones that Mother had told about the sporting life here in the early 1900s, and I was halfway to buying the corks to dangle from my hat, but it did not happen.

About this time in June I was suddenly told that Master John was not well and would not be coming into the office in the immediate future. I was asked by Mrs Boardman to take certain papers round to him to sign and when I said words to the effect that I expected that he would soon be back he replied, "I do not know when that will be, Neil." He died on 21st July 1962. I remember going to the Young Farmers that evening but all I could think of was Mrs Boardman and "What will happen now?"

CHAPTER 6

Deceit From a Friend

T he very first thing that happened was that Jack Webb spent several evenings on his own when no one was about, up in the attic clearing out loads and loads of papers. What they were I have no idea, but I guessed that he was hiding something because after this he vacated the office never to come in again. About the same time Mr Geoffrey Boardman, John's brother, called at the office. He said, "I am the executor of John's estate and we would like you to carry on as manager for the time being" and then added, "The partners of Boardman and Oliver have kindly offered to help." Boardman and Oliver were a sort of a sister firm, in that the young Paul Oliver had started with Mr Charles Boardman, firstly in Haverhill, then they had jointly opened the practice in Sudbury. Paul Oliver's son Rowley was now the senior partner, then Ted Eady and Ray Emeny, the youngest. All of them duly came over once at different times. Ted Eady had been one of Mother's old dance partners, so of course he filled me in on that. Ray took the auction of the old Haverhill police station, and Rowley, the senior partner, advised in an agricultural matter.

Geoffrey Boardman then said, "We are going to buy a house in Beaumont Court for Molly," who was John's widow, "as the council wishes to acquire Burton Cottage." He continued, "We have had an enquiry from an estate agent wanting to purchase the place lock, stock and barrel, but if you are interested we will let you buy the business for £5,500. This represents £2,000 for the freehold and £3,500 for the goodwill." I chatted this offer over with Mother, who agreed with me that £3,500 for the goodwill was grossly excessive, as this declining business had no goodwill, just a little scope. Geoffrey said that they would discount the price by £500 for me, but I still did not feel confident enough to have a go, so I phoned an old Grain and Chalk employee who had bought his office from them. "Of course Neil, I will be pleased to help and advise you. Come down to my house for a chat."

Later when I arrived at his house there was another ex-Grain and Chalk employee, who had also left the firm to start on his own, and they both greeted me like a long-lost friend and we all shook hands. They made me feel that I was amongst friends, so I told them all I knew about the firm and what I thought I could do with it, and answered every question that they asked, thinking that they were both on my side and would honestly advise me in my pursuit to buy it for myself. They said nothing more to me only that they would be in touch.

The following day they approached Geoffrey Boardman, saying that the two of them would like to come and inspect the property with a view to buying the firm for themselves. Having told them everything that I knew thinking that they were going to help me, I was livid and when I told Geoffrey Boardman he seemed to be a bit on my side, saying, "Let them come and see it first." I kept well out of the way when they came, knowing that I would only express myself if I saw them. The thought of this double-cross incensed me, and I was ready for battle, if battle it be. I understand that the ex-Grain and Chalk pair did put an offer in and the other enquirer, who also came to have a look, said that they were no longer interested. Not long after this my former colleague came to our office to obtain the keys to do a mortgage valuation. In parking his new car against a high kerb he scratched it all along one side, then came into our office in a fury shouting "Neil" at the top of his voice as if it was my fault. In the whole of my career I only saw him once more and that was much later in the vice-president's marquee at the Suffolk Agricultural Show, where I was stewarding. I was on my own and for this I was wearing a smart dark grey suit, white shirt and bowler hat. We recognised each other instantly and without speaking he gave me a long blank stare, which for me said it all.

To his credit Geoffrey Boardman, who was a pensive pipe smoker, came down the office to see me, saying, "We would like you to carry on managing the business for the time being. For our part we will have a new front door made and the window onto The Pightle opened up, and the office given a coat of paint." Harold Onion, the joiner next door in Station Road, duly came and did exactly as he had said, which was well pleasing. Geoffrey also said that John had made no more than £500 a year out of the business and Mrs Boardman would be happy with the same.

Jack Webb immediately announced his retirement, as he thought that he should have been made manager, and although he only lived in walking distance away in Chantry Road, he never came nigh me or by me. Geoffrey found a replacement for Jack Webb in a Mr Leslie Parkin who he had known for some years. Mr Parkin had a club foot which made it difficult for him to get about. He too had tales of old Haverhill, one being that as he walked to school across the Downs early morning the place was alive with the rattle of the looms in the sheds on the allotments of people doing outwork weaving for Gurteen's clothing factory. The whole place, he said, seemed to rely on the weaving trade and weavers' houses still exist to this day in Upper Downs Slade and Burton End. Each house had three floors: the family lived on the bottom floor and slept on the top, and the middle floor was one big room where the loom would be worked continuously by all the family.

I sold by auction a block of four building plots in Bridewell Street, Clare, in December. I took Les Parkin with me and as this was the first freehold property that I had ever sold by auction, I was as nervous as a kitten. I wrote every word that I intended to say on the cover of my particulars and, according to Les, I went like a train. I nevertheless got through OK.

We hardly had a house for sale and the lady who then lived in Mr Charles Boardman's old house, Abbott's Hall, Sturmer, had taken her business to an Ipswich agent who, on finding that he could not move it, offered it to ourselves on a half-commission if you sell it basis. It was a very fashionable property and out of the blue we had a telephone enquiry for it. I nervously took the call, asking the very well-spoken lady for her address. "Fwog End Fwarm," she said. Now me, being an old country boy, was not used to this town accent and I asked her again to no avail. At the third time of no success I asked her how to spell it. "F war o g," she said. Anyway she and her husband bought the property.

About this time I also did a full tenant-right changeover sale at Wood Ditton where the valuer's assistant had been older than me and appeared in breeches. Again this job was something that I had watched and never done before on my own. The valuer for the in-goer came from King's Lynn, so we agreed to meet at a suitable hostelry that was situated about halfway, in order to finalise and agree valuations. This was on a Monday. I had been away for the weekend and completely forgot, so I agreed another date at his office in King's Lynn and got the business done. Mr Charles Boardman had got on well for the East of England Co-op and seemed to get most of their work in East Anglia. At the annual valuation for income tax purposes, for Enfield Highway Co-op at Holyfield Hall Farm, Waltham Abbey, I nervously arrived and had an excellent lunch with the manager, Philip Craven, and his good lady. After lunch we went out to value the growing crop of potatoes and Mr Craven asked me what I thought the yield might be. On hearing that they were King Edwards I tentatively suggested

14 tons an acre. "Hm," said Mr Craven as he dug up a root, then another root, then another and at this point he said, "The average number of potatoes that will keep within a two-inch riddle will be the average tonnage per acre." I had not heard of this before, but rule-of-thumb measurements such as this were right up my street.

Philip was interested in all sorts of Yorkshire rural life and folk-lore and he told me about Nine Men's Morris, something else that had gone on all around me and that I was not aware of. Rules-of-thumb like the potatoes have always interested me, and I remember when I was studying forestry for my final exam phoning the Forestry Commission at Tangham Forest, asking if anyone there would give a bit of advice. An old forester took me out to measure the height of a tree. No, I am not climbing that, I thought, being ignorant of the easier way which was to use the right-angle triangle principle. By this one would take an arm-length twig and hold it between thumb and forefinger in an outstretched arm, then swing the twig upright so that the distance from eye to forefinger and forefinger to top of vertical twig would be the same. On matching the upright twig to the usable height of the trunk, the distance between yourself and the base of the tree would be the same as the usable height.

I always found anything to do with measurement interesting and had often wondered how on earth the old farmworkers knew how many beans were needed to fill a bean barrow to plough in across a field. In the fourteenth century, a furlong or furrow length was 40 perches and there were eight furlongs to a mile. A stetch pole was eight foot three inches and in streets of this age half a rod or 16 foot six inches was the width of a plot of land that a house in a street was allowed to stand on. My Grandfather had farmed two farms, these being the Red House and the Hollies Farm, where he lived at Wicker Street Green, Kersey, which amounted to 280 acres which was still more or less in line with the Domesday Book where it was deemed that 120–140 acres was suitable for a family.

This had been the size of the majority of farms when I was with Spears, but modern mechanisation has changed all that. At Spears I remember us doing a valuation against an ancient valuer from Beccles, who would talk about going on tenant-right valuations with his father, who would settle the amount to be paid by the incomer there and then if it took all night, and sometimes it did. Only then was the incomer allowed onto the land and to do that he had to pay over the cash first. At tenant-right valuations done in Norfolk and Suffolk the tenant had rights of holdover after vacating to enter and thresh corn, and it was the tradition that stover (clover hay) should be left free for the in-goer. I loved and marvelled at these stories of the olden days and imagined how they were the forerunner of what we were doing then in the days before the modern technological revolution and all its alleged advantages which has, incidentally, taken away much of the skill and technique of the individual.

I used to attend the Chartered Auctioneers Suffolk Junior section meetings and when they could not get anyone to stand as secretary I agreed to do the job. We had some memorable after-dinner speakers including Merrick Griffiths, the Newmarket auctioneer talking about the turf and his business, much of which revolved around horseracing and its people. Sam Flick of Saxmundham made his evening particularly interesting, arranging for us all to do a mock agricultural tenant-right valuation. We duly met at a prearranged farm at Earl Soham where he divided everyone up into pairs, of which one was to act for the out-goer and the other the in-goer. He told us that even those who only did urban work could benefit. We were all given sheets of instruction as to what we had to value and then we all retired to the local pub, The Falcon, which has long since closed, to work it all out over a pint and a ploughman's.

Sam Flick had of course been our main competitor when I was at Spears, where I was a bit scared of him, but he provided us with a magnificent instructive evening that was as good as I have ever been to anywhere. I well remember him telling us that whilst farmyard manure was valued at 27 cubic feet or a cubic yard to the ton, when it was in the yard if you valued it when it had been removed to the heap one should allow 40 cubic feet to the ton as it will have expanded.

On another occasion, with his son Tony Flick, I judged a chartered surveyors' auctioneering contest. Roger Pasco was chairman of our Suffolk Junior Auctioneers, and we had a lot of fun. Roger and I had to attend the annual meeting of our junior section in London and along with many other regional groups put a proposition for something or other. Roger got up and gave a magnificent proposal. I was supposed to second this with three reasons why. It was, however, in the middle of a sleepy afternoon and after a heavy lunch and with my usual nerves I got up and said, "I have nothing further to add to what my chairman has said" and sat down. Roger forgave my uselessness at this sort of thing.

Although I was now a qualified and elected Fellow of the Royal Institute of Chartered Surveyors, which had amalgamated with the Chartered Auctioneers, I cannot think of any knowledge at all that I gained for all the time in study, sweat, labour and burning the midnight oil that I took in passing their exams. There was certainly nothing at all considered about how to conduct an auction sale, the bidding, and above all my personally discovered winning secret – the psychology coupled with discovering Kipling's honest serving men.

I discussed with Mother what I thought that I should do as to whether I might buy the business or risk losing it. Things had picked up and I felt a bit more confident. So she said, "Go and see what they say", so as young and lacking in confidence as I was, I did just that and Mother and I worked out a plan of action. On 15th February 1963 I went to see Mr Geoffrey, asking if I could buy the business after all. I had lost my £500 discount, and he would not budge, but when I asked if I could complete at the end of the year and have for myself everything over the £500 that Mrs Boardman needed for the year, he accepted. I then upped the value of the freehold property to £3,500 and arranged an 80% mortgage with the Eastern Counties Building Society. Mother agreed to stand guarantor at the bank for the rest, but she need not have worried, for when the end of the year and completion came round I had earned enough money to pay for it.

"Enthusiasm is the quality that guarantees all others" – R.W. Emerson.

The first person to congratulate me was Bob Grain, and how he knew I shall never know. He must have followed my progress very carefully, as indeed did Michael Spear, because he was a Mason and I had reports back that he had met Eric Baldock, the proprietor of my local garage at a dinner and he had wanted to know how I was getting on. "Would you like to come back and sell for me, again?" asked Bob Grain. "You bet," I thought to myself. This really put me on the front foot as I could get no more prestigious recognition than this. Cambridge farm machinery sales were the largest of their kind in Europe, and loads of farmers local to Boardman's would attend. I knew that there were a lot of auctioneers at Grain and Chalk and to put me in front of them was a marvellous boost. This would really put me in the picture. It meant a great deal to me and clearly my progress meant something to him.

At this time I used to phone my Mother every night. It was the first thing that I did when I got into bed. She had experienced, in the agricultural depression and in losing Father, more things than I ever could, and although I did not always agree with her, I found someone as experienced in life and business as she was, immeasurable. By the time she died, from a standing start she had bought and sold 50 houses.

Not everyone was on my side though and there were those who would exploit my lack of experience for their own good. A local accountant said that he had a query on one of our farmer client's annual valuations for income tax, and asked if he could see my valuation book where I had taken details. He took the book away with him, although he gave it back to me later. The next year when I phoned the farmer for an appointment as usual to do his annual tax valuation, he told me that I was not required as his accountant was going to do it. I said he can't do it properly, but he still went with the accountant. When I told Ray Emeny of Oliver's, he said, "Never let anyone see inside your valuation book. It is your opinion and a secret. That is why we all have codes." He was right of course, and I knew because 'that which hurts teaches'.

Another auctioneer's assistant that I spoke to said that as a pupil at tenant-right valuations it was his job to break the code of the opposing valuer. Peter Grain's had been 'take up crib' where 't' equals one, 'u' would be two and 'b' nought. I think that I am safe in revealing that because there is but little professional work done now in this modern age. A dealer friend said that he had cracked the code on the sale tickets of a big antique dealer in Long Melford and his was 'show-market'. Knowing other valuers' codes was important because, like estimates in the saleroom, it is amazing how much people's personal opinions as to value differ when not influenced by others. Other valuers' opinions, if higher than one thought, can be attacked and hopefully brought down, but if it is lower than yours you leave it alone and keep quiet. I used Peter Grain's and I remember being in an antique shop with John Tasker when he said to me in front of the proprietor, "Do you think that Thomas Underwood would like it?" Of course we knew no such person of this name but I knew that he meant, "I will offer him £15 for it" – T being 1 and U being 5. Thank goodness this did not graduate to the auction room as I would not have known where I was.

A client of the firm had gone to Balls and Balls, the agents of Sible Hedingham, to sell his farm. I heard rumours about it beforehand and called to see him. I was not asked in, and he told me on the doorstep that the matter was out of his hands. Claude Spear would attend other people's auctions, so on the day of the sale I got myself up in my best suit and waistcoat with winged collar that Mother had

got a tailor to make for me. It was in a fine grey-blue houndstooth remnant that Mother had bought at a market, and despite this I fancied myself in it.

At the auction I stood at the back, when who should come in and stand next to me but about the only person that I could have recognised, a Mrs Florence Crossman. I had only seen her once before but knew that she was a property developer in a large way and that she drove a gull-winged Mercedes. I put all nervousness aside and confidently introduced myself and asked her about some development that she was going to do in Haverhill. "Oh," she said, "we have already spoken to Grahams about that, so I am afraid that it is too late." We then chatted about a few property matters, with me trying to sound as informed as I could. Grahams were the only other agents in Haverhill then, and had taken almost all of our property business, and thus were our sworn enemy, in spite of politeness when we met. Mrs Crossman then said, "We are going round to our solicitors, Cunningham, Son and Orfeur. Would you care to come?" Why she should say this I have no idea, but I duly went, then said goodbye. I really think that it was my best Sunday go meeting suit that did it and needless to say we were ultimately instructed as sole agents on Mrs Crossman's Haverhill development.

Mr Boardman had been the secretary of the Haverhill Corn Exchange Company, so after his death, I was asked if I would take it on. The first time that I met the chairman and committee members was in our Haverhill office. Again I was as nervous as a kitten. Mr

Ernest Unwin, the chairman, was an enormous man and I could hardly hold his overcoat. He brought with him his two sons, F St G Unwin and Colonel Jim who had played rugby for England. I blurted out in an erratic stupor the minutes of the last meeting, which John Boardman had written. There was not much else to report, but Owen Mynott, who was present, let it be known that he would be pleased to buy any unwanted shares, which he did in due course, and which proved to be a good investment when the place was later sold to the Haverhill Urban District Council. Anyway I was enjoying my new-found responsibilities and the extraordinary idiosyncrasies of most of the people.

CHAPTER 7

Some Scams, Jokes and Tricks

I had not been in Haverhill very long when I was asked to go back to East Suffolk to conduct an auction following a harvest festival service to be held in a public house – The Lion at Little Glemham. I agreed to do it and asked all my old mates from the Young Farmers to come for a good night out. The vicar duly held the service, then it was my turn to conduct a sale of the produce that had been given. For this I stood on a beer crate behind the bar. After I had made my usual silly announcement of "The highest bidder to be the buyer unless anyone bids more!" we started the auction, but where were my Young Farmer mates? It seems that they had been scared of the religious part, so they came through the door just as I was in action, and I took bids off them although they had not bid. I was knocking them down a bunch of carrots here for 18 pence and a marrow there for a shilling or so, for which they all played their part and begrudgingly paid up, in spite of not bidding. The last lot of the evening was a bunch of Michaelmas daisies which would not have made a bob in the market. The bidding surprisingly opened at two shillings, then went up and up with bids coming from a voice in the back room behind me, against my mate in front who had bought the carrots. Finally I knocked the lot down to the bidder who had shouted from the back room, at the extraordinary price of 19 shillings. "Who was that?" I cried. To which there was no reply, so I had to get down from my beer crate to go into the back room where I found that the buyer was my marrow-acquiring mate who replied to my "Who bought that lot?" question with "We know that as an auctioneer you cannot bid so we were bidding for you. You've got to pay the 19 shillings for the Michaelmas daisies!"

There was always much banter in the saleroom. Somehow that fun seems to have been killed off when bidding numbers were instigated. I remember a Mr Matthews laboriously calling out his name whenever he had bought a lot and always adding "two ts" until someone shouted "with milk and sugar?"

There was a famous old auctioneer from Framlingham named Alfred Preston. Apparently a horse dealer had been giving him some gyp. When the dealer went to look in a horse's mouth to see how old it was, he said "You want to look up the other end, you might learn something." Another horse auctioneer had said to some dealers who seemed to be ganging together, "You hang together like pawn brokers' balls."

In our saleroom, Peter, one of our porters, had been on the door checking everyone out with their lots when a very smart-looking young lady went out carrying a tiny games table. Now at this time Lenny, an old Suffolk boy who worked for the carriers, went past and said, "What a lovely little piece that is, Pete," to which Peter duly replied and I won't say the rest but those two old rascals were talking about her and not the table and she did not realise it.

It is amazing what goes through your head in the heat of the moment when you are on the rostrum. A man called Nelson called his name out and had to call it twice as I couldn't hear. Without thinking, off the back brain I said, "I know, spelt with one eye."

A dealer called Graham Lower was a regular at our sales and after he had bought something would call his name out after each lot he bought. One time when he shouted out his name – "Lower" – I said without thinking and hesitation, "Sorry sir it can't be any lower." He was the only one to see the joke and we exchanged knowing smiles.

People were warned against dealing with the dealer who comes unannounced knocking at the door, but there used to be a man who wore a funny pompom hat who would say "Morning madam. I'm in the area buying pianos and today I can give £200 for any piano." Now no end of people at that time of day had a piano from grandma's day left over that they would be glad to get rid of anyhow. In fact at local fetes they even had piano-breaking competitions. There were loads of people who would do anything to get rid of that damned thing that took up all the space, so they would invite 'pompom hat' inside to see it. He would run his fingers knowingly along the keyboard, then say, "Yes, that's fine madam, I'll have that. Now I can also give a very good price for corner cupboards," and anything else he had seen out of the corner of his eye. Then he would talk the good lady into letting him up into the attic and outside in the shed, where all the damaged period pieces are often found, and then make out a list for the things that he could carry, which would be everything except the piano. He would then pay and take those items saying, "I cannot manage the piano on my own, but Fred and Jim will be along next week and they will pay you then." There used to be loads of people about with a £200 piano that they could never sell!

There was a story going round that 'Pompom' had bought a clock on one of these occasions that was inscribed on the dial, Edward, East London, but he could find no maker called Edward of East London. So he had moved it on cheaply, only to find out later that it was by Edward East of London, who is arguably this country's finest clock-maker, which made the clock extremely valuable.

SOME SCAMS, JOKES AND TRICKS

It was rumoured that at one of the market sales, that would pay out during a sale, a local dealer, who was going bad, had emptied a large proportion of his antique stock into the sale, for it to be mostly bought by an unknown buyer who had disappeared after the sale without paying and leaving any knowledge of his name or address. Meanwhile the dealer had been paid out immediately after the sale.

It was usual to give livestock dealers a week's credit in cattle markets. For example, if the sale was held on a Monday the usual arrangement was for the cheque for this Monday would arrive for last Monday's purchases. A new prospective purchaser with a Smithfield address wrote and asked for this arrangement and engaged a well-known local livestock buyer to do their bidding. This worked well for the first six months. Then they got a week behind in paying. By the time that they got a third week behind, the auctioneers smelt a rat and got someone in London to call upon them, where they found a one-room fifth-floor office with no more than a desk, a chair and a disconnected telephone.

A furniture dealer bought a house full of forty paintings by an artist called Batchelder for £200 the lot. He then advertised under a box number in the local papers that £100 each would be paid for paintings by Batchelder. Having done this he distributed them into salerooms far and wide and there seemed a greatly increased demand for work by this artist but there were several people who wondered why it was that they did not get a reply to the advertisement box number!

There used to be a lovely old Norfolk boy from Wymondham by the name of Bunn who would come to the sale, and guess what, he was a baker and he usually brought the girls a bag of his cakes. On this particular day during the sale I saw him move to stand near a longcase clock, so I guessed that he was going to bid for it. Now it is a standard trick that crafty people will try to knock you down just as you are about to sell the lot by asking a question such as, "Have you got the piece that's missing?" or "Have you got the key?" or something negative, so I had decided that if anyone pulled this trick on me with a downer in front of the assembled company, whatever the circumstances, I would always answer "Yes," then qualify it even if the answer was in effect "No." Sure enough, as soon as the lot number was mentioned, "Does it work sir?" cried Mr Bunn. Now that was a telling question, for whilst I knew nothing wrong with it, if I had said "Yes" then I could be made responsible for whatever may have needed to be done to it, so he knew that I would have to say, I don't know, which could have put doubts in people's minds, so I replied, "Yes, that can be made to work." He never forgot it and reminded me every time that I saw him. It made me wonder how many times he had got away with it in sunny Norfolk!

From the rostrum it was possible to actually make people bid. I discovered that private people would drop out of the bidding for lack of confidence and that it was possible to get them to bid again if you gave them a reassuring smile and a nod which never failed. People would sometimes bid in peculiar ways, so that others in the saleroom do not know that they were bidding. I surmised that this is because others will run them up and this gives them a safe feeling. Some cattle market dealers would keep their bidding secret by standing behind the auctioneer and poking him in the back, and another would have secret signals prearranged with the auctioneer such as holding the lapel of his jacket if he wanted to bid again. An independent London lady dealer would try to hide herself up behind big pieces of furniture when bidding. An American auctioneer that I met told me that when holding sales in a marquee at private houses he would always have an opening on one side left so that he could see the coffee bar and, if possible, the same on the other side with an open view to the toilets from where, he assured me, he would always get bids. We once sold a very early Gothic oak chest that had been sent to a London saleroom by a certain ancient West Country monastery as it was surplus to their requirements. It had not realised a very high price and the dealer who bought it decided to put it in one of our oak sales. We were told that we could use its provenance and duly advertised it with these details to find that a solicitor came and bought it, we understood, on behalf of a wealthy benefactor whose intention was to give it back to the monastery!

Our only development of new residential houses for sale at this time had been the last of a small estate on the Downs in Haverhill. Our competitors had the rest. I was desperate to get a foothold in new property sales but all that was about to change.

CHAPTER 8

The Turn of the Tide

One day a big rough and ready looking man with flame red hair and an open-neck shirt called at the office and asked if we had any building land. I used to sit in Mr Boardman's office and at his desk. I kept the door ajar so I could hear all that was going on in the front office and, at the words 'building land', I roared out to speak to the caller, whose name I was to learn was Douglas Leach. I knew the importance of selling building land to developers because it was usual for them to instruct the agent that they had bought the land from in the sale of the houses that they were to erect. We only had two small plots of land for sale, but I managed to get Douglas in my car to see them, where I knew we could have a chat. He did not tell me all, but word on the grapevine told me that he had been to Australia and had come back with a few hundred pounds with which he had bought a small chicken farm and subsequently obtained permission for one dwelling thereon. It was reputed that the local builders' merchant had then persuaded him to build the dwelling himself, by having materials on credit from themselves and employing separate contractors for all of the trades, which he did. Having done that and sold the house, he bought another site for two and then never looked back. He had expanded and expanded and now had a big estate at Kedington which was about four miles from Haverhill.

I did not sell him anything but was desperate to find something for him and he would often call at the office. The Boardman family owned a plot for eight houses off Crowland Road in Haverhill, and as soon as they agreed to put them on the market I offered them to Douglas, who immediately said that he would have them. The plans and prices for the new houses were prepared, but when I went onto the site to take further details, a 'clever' site worker said "You aren't getting 'em, they are going to your rivals." I phoned Douglas, who said of the other agents, "They must hate you but don't worry, I will make it right." And so he did with instructions on a host of one, two and four bungalow plots, mainly at out of the way places such as Shelfanger and Westhorpe which were far away, near Diss in Norfolk, and also Stanningfield and other sites which in the expanding climate of the mid-1960s all sold very quickly.

We found that it was difficult for us to compete and sell residential property on the more expensive London and Cambridge side of Haverhill but not so going north or east where we could compete with anyone. We still had no large estates although we did sell a few bungalows in Ashen near Clare for a small Essex developer.

Out of the blue Mr Leach phoned one day to say, "Would you care to sell the houses on my estate at Kedington?" I had heard on the grapevine that he was a bit fed up with his other agent, who had let a prospective buyer walk the four miles to Kedington and walk the four miles back again to their Haverhill office. Buses were few in those days, but you should never let such a thing happen. "Thank you very much," was my reply, and I instantly set about it. The Greater London Council had recently announced a scheme for people in certain central London areas whereby they would give 100% loans on private houses, regardless of personal income, so we advertised these houses in the *Evening Standard*, the *Evening News*, the *Walthamstow Gazette* and *Tottenham and Edmonton Weekly Herald* at the modest price of "from £2,995", and put a rep on site over the weekend. This rep happened to be my sister Audrey, and of course Mother came too. I can still hear Mother saying, "There is another one here," as Audrey took no less than 15 deposits. Douglas was delighted and other estates were to follow.

I remember that at this time a black person called Harry Braithwaite came down from London and he asked me if there was any prejudice in the area. "No," I said for there was hardly anyone to be prejudiced about at that time in Suffolk, and if anything they were interesting for their difference. He then paid a deposit and subsequently purchased one of Douglas Leach's houses. When, later, I saw him working on Douglas's site we exchanged knowing smiles and it gave me great pleasure as I felt that I had done the right thing.

There were four shops on the site at Kedington at this time and the last one on the corner was sold to a would-be newsagent, who could not get any daily papers supplied to him try as he might. A mate of mine, who was also a newsagent, explained that the unions were very strong in the print business and would not let anyone new in. Douglas said, "Can you do anything to help him Neil?" I would have done anything for Douglas Leach, who had put us on the property map, so I advertised in the local paper for a newspaper round and duly bought one in Hundon, the next village for not much more than a few quid, and so I was able to secure the supply of newspapers to the shop in Kedington. One up to the Arsenal!

Mrs Crossman's houses in Beaumont vale were a bit on the expensive side, proving difficult to move, and the market had slowed, so one weekend we advertised that a rep would be on site. When I went down to see how it was going, there was an agent from London with his brochures all over the place and ours somewhat sidelined. I had heard about this guy and how his aggressive tactics had been successful, but

I was not going to give him the easy ride that he may have been getting elsewhere on my patch. I knew that he would try and stir it up for us and he left saying that he was going to do just that, but to my surprise I had a phone call from Mr Enticknap, the secretary to the Crossman Development Company, who said that we were one of the few agents that had played ball with them and this agent would not be selling these properties any longer. One nil to the Arsenal!

In our front office, Margaret, the typist/secretary/teamaker and above all else a humourist, was as sharp as they come. A prospective purchaser had viewed a property through our competitors that we had for sale as well, and thinking that she was phoning our competitors to buy it but she had actually phoned ourselves. Margaret chatted to her and then got her to come to our office, and soon took the deposit and we then instructed solicitors.

On another occasion a vendor intending to instruct both agents had instructed our competitors first. When we heard this we knew that the others had been given enough time to get details into their advertisement in the *Haverhill Echo* which would come out the next morning. It was now four o'clock and whilst I went to take particulars, Margaret got all envelopes ready for prospective purchasers so that we could get the particulars in the post that night. Needless to say, we sold this property at 9am the next morning. I enjoyed this time a lot as with only two people involved in the selling, we both knew all that was going on and could be 100% efficient. I found, as we grew larger, that this was no longer to be the case, and the estate agency, apart from just making money, gradually became less enjoyable.

Reps were calling and saying that instead of the old hand model gestetner, a duplicator system was coming out whereby we would be able to print a black and white photo on our particulars. If you know what the gestetner was like, then you would think this unbeliev-able. What this involved was a Rotaprint A4 size offset-litho printer, which reproduced by transferring an oil-based ink image onto a water-dampened revolving blanket, which then in turn offset this onto the paper. Now comes the clever bit. The property would be photographed with a large Polaroid Land Camera which gave one an instant black and clear positive, broken by a screen into minute dots for the image. This in turn would be cut into the paper particulars for printing, then transferred to a metal plate for the Rotaprint. It cost about £800, which was all of my second year's profit, but it really put us on the map. We were the first estate agents in East Anglia to have this and we could now make our auction catalogues a lot better, as well as our property particulars. It really was a revolution for us.

The estate agency side was going great guns and we now had loads of modestly priced new estates of bungalows and houses. I noticed how people loved filling in forms, so I had professionally designed a handwritten scroll with the price in bold black "from £2,725" and a dotted edge and scissors for cutting out, and lines for name and address. We had the cheapest area within 50 miles of London and this unusual ad was a real puller.

I did not smoke but my Mother had given me a little walnut ciga-rette box with the initial 'L' on it. I kept it on my desk full of cigarettes so that I could hand them round to clients. But I noticed that the level kept getting lower for no reason, so when there was only about three cigarettes left, I rolled up a piece of cardboard and wrote on it, "Now smoke this." I soon found out that the two culprits were Maureen, my secretary, and Jean Delaney who was in charge of the printing.

Similarly, I acquired a little snuff box with an inscription on it as to how it was made out of the wreck of the *Royal George*, which had been sunk at Spithead. I filled it up with fresh snuff and waited and waited for George Jackson to come in as he was my only snuff-taking client. When he eventually took a pinch he coughed and spluttered saying it was too damp. Apparently I had waited too long.

Now that I had a little jingle in my pockets I used to have my suits made to measure by Mr Leadbeater, the cutter at Gurteen's

Haverhill clothing factory, and he would deliver them to the office. I was out one time, and someone opened the door to my office to find my secretary doing her Barbra Streisand act, singing and dancing off the chairs dressed in my new suit. She was an excellent secretary nonetheless, and as fierce in business as I was, I pride myself in the fact that they knew that they could kick over the traces occasionally.

There was an agent in Clare called Mattingly and Clowes. They did more architectural things than sell houses, but it was rumoured that they were closing. Their small shop was at the start of the Market Place in Well Lane and just right for an estate agent's office. Having phoned David Winch, a partner in Wayman and Long, the long-standing Clare solicitors, to get the gen, I agreed with Mattingly and Clowes to take on the lease. The landlady, Joyce Parker, who owned a lot of property in Clare, seemed delighted that we were to open. Margaret Sadler was keen to manage the office on her own and all properties could be inspected by someone from the Haverhill Office. It worked well and we seemed to get nearly all of the Clare residential house sales.

Although work such as public house valuations dropped off, and I refused to let lettings get in my way, I tried hard to keep up the agricultural side, particularly the farm sales. I remember one almost as soon as I took over, which was at Great Lodge Farm, Hundon, for Arthur Bass. Justin Brook was taking over and would no doubt be covering it with fruit trees. It is where Adrian Bell had worked when he first arrived in Suffolk, and I felt that it was an excellent advertisement for the new regime.

Boardmans did a large number of farmers' annual valuations for income tax purposes and I am proud to say that we only lost two following my takeover. There seemed to be a lot of Robin Hoodism in our charges and the small farmers were charged next to nothing. These were your annual visit to the farm and most farmers' wives made sure that you were welcomed with a piece or two of shortcake or similar. Farmers such as Tom Blackmore from College Farm, Horseheath, who farmed his 80 acres on his own with a little help where and when he could get it. The Corn Exchanges had closed by now and Tom was getting fed up with reps constantly disturbing him when he wanted to get on, so he hung in the farmyard a sign reading 'Callers strictly only by appointment'.

Tom's boy Bugsy was just coming up to school-leaving age and Tom needed a hand, so he kept Bugsy away from school for a couple of days to help him. When Bugsy returned, Tom sent a note telling the truth of exactly what had happened. About two days later there was a screech of brakes in Tom's farmyard and a school inspector in a pinstripe suit got out of his car saying, "Mr Blackmore, I want a word with you. You have been keeping your son away from school against the law. Don't you want him to learn to read and write?" "Can you read?" said Tom. "Of course I can read," said Pinstripe, "No you can't," said Tom, "because if you could read you would have read my sign that says 'Callers strictly only by appointment'. Now be off with you."

As I found that I was generating more work than I could personally handle, I was pleased when Eric Fretwell from Ely said that he would give me a hand. He had been a pupil with A T Grain and Sons at Ely and had passed his exams. He had left Grains to start his own piggery and having fed his pigs each day now had some time on his hands to come and do some professional work for us. He took on all work relating to three massive plant and machinery auctions that we held for W C French, acting on behalf of the Greater London Council at Witham, Huntingdon and Haverhill, and other more general professional work. It was nevertheless the residential property side that was something that we expanded on, doubling and trebling the turnover each year. At the same time our antique sales seemed to grow and grow.

Eric went out one day to take on for sale a property in Helions Bumpstead which is a few yards from the position where three counties meet – Essex, Suffolk and Cambridgeshire. On seeing the photograph, I had to go and have a look at this sixteenth-century timbered cottage and decided there and then that I wanted to buy it, which I did. The vendor, Mr Brown, was a retired London policeman and had been selling it at £3,000 to a purchaser who had been unable to raise a mortgage on this old unmodernised property. I loved it, and thinking that it was worth more than Brown's price I duly gave him £500 extra, as I wanted an answer to the tittle-tattle that anyone might make out of me, an estate agent, buying it for myself. As we say in Suffolk, "Half the lies you hear are not true" and I wanted a reply to all the rubbish that was starting to follow whatever I did. I raised an 80% mortgage through the Halifax Building Society, who were more relaxed about older property, and it became my home for nearly 40 years.

'Ivy Todd' was the name of my timbered and plain-tiled former farmhouse that stood in just under an acre on a corner at Drapers Green in this unspoilt area. As soon as I had finished having the house modernised, I moved in on my own and Mother immediately said, "I'll come over and sort the house out for you. You'll need to buy a good-sized deep freeze." Which I did. She stayed for over a week and did not mind being on her own during the day as she kept herself busy. At the office in Haverhill I would get phone calls from her saying that she had bought such and such, and would I call at the butcher's to pick these joints up on the way home. I remember one of the butchers wanting to know about her. I think that she had impressed him by knowing all of the various cuts of meat that were the best value. There would be as many as six Argentine joints of rib for the freezer which she would bone out, remove some of the fat and roll and tie, and also some particular pork joints which, being at the end of the hand and an odd shape, were usually about half the price of the normal shaped joint.

Mother also sorted out the curtains and similarly provided the bed linen and made for me a little needlework pocket for pins, needles and spare buttons etc. She saw to it that I would be in the 'Land Goshen', as she put it, in the language used in the tin chapel she had attended as a child.

It never ceased to amaze me the things that Mother knew. If we went out for a walk at night Mother knew the name of all the major stars and constellations in the sky. I attributed this to the fact that when in her youth she had been out hunting she was often left with six miles or more to hack back home across country and she would do that by following the byways that she knew guided by the stars. She would in turn point out the Pole Star, the Milky Way, the Seven Sisters and the Plough – she could read signs of the forthcoming weather from it. One being: "When the moon is on its back it holds the water in its lap." How much have we lost by losing our observational eye to become replaced by dead pedagogy, I ask?

I remember Mother shouting, "Come and look at this." It was the aurora borealis and she knew all about it. On a similar occasion, it was the planes of soldiers towing gliders to Arnhem, towards the end of the war. You may think that knowing about the stars is irrelevant to auctioneering. Not so – all this background knowledge stored from observation was of importance and proved to be so when we sold such things as an Orrery (a working model of the stars). Believe you me, everything counts.

About the time that I had bought Ivy Todd, I used to go to football matches with a friend from Newmarket who was a bit older than me. He phoned one Saturday morning saying would I meet him at the Wagon and Horses at Newmarket early that evening and would say nothing more, not even where we were going, and he made it a complete mystery, other than to just get in the car.

"Head for Cambridge," said my Newmarket friend, "I have fixed up the Mother and daughter combination." He had mentioned this 'combination' some time before, but I thought that he was joking as usual. We pulled up outside a smart modern house in Girton on the

My wife Hazel.

outskirts of Cambridge. On opening the front door the first thing that I noticed was the large antique Afghan carpet in the lounge, and joked to myself "that will do as a dowry" not knowing that this wayward thought was to come to reality. I was pleasantly surprised when introduced to Hazel who I found was quite a looker, and I learned from my colleague that she had just separated from her husband and was fairly cut up one way and another. We had a pleasant dinner together in St Ives, and agreed to do the same again the following week. It took Hazel a long time to get her old self back, but I stuck in there and as Nat King Cole said in his ballad 'September Song', "I played me a waiting game and as time came along she came my way." It seemed ironic that that having only just acquired my nest I immediately found a suitable nest mate.

Hazel stood only five foot, two inches tall, but I was to discover that she was a pocket battleship on the sports field. She had attended the Perse Ladies School in Cambridge where she had played for the county girls' team at both tennis and hockey and was to captain the newly formed Haverhill ladies hockey team. She was not working when I first met her, but when things settled she found a suitable position as the secretary to the area manager of the Trustee Savings Bank in Cambridge, where she stayed until we married. On a holiday in France, Hazel whose looks were what I called 'the Brigitte Bardot pout' was pursued by Frenchmen, and I literally had to fight them off. One who was very determined kept asking me questions and what her name meant in English. When I told him 'nut' he went away exclaiming "Un noix! Un noix?" Later she gave birth to our twins George and Kate, and as soon as they were at school she came back into the business with me.

Meeting John Tasker was a boon and it came through my sister Audrey. She had been with a friend to the Grand National horserace at Aintree and on the way home had stopped at a small antique shop in Uppingham. This was run by John, who, when she told him that her brother was an auctioneer, had said, "If he ever has a private house sale where he can take in extra lots please let me know." Shortly after this we had a suitable occasion of a marquee sale at a large house at Kedington, and the vendor agreed to us bringing in a few extra lots as this would help with our commission charges. It was a known thing that prices at a private house sale would generally well exceed those achieved in a collective sale. John sent down about six lots, including a pocket-sized silver singing bird automata which made about three times his reserve, and the other lots sold similarly. He then decided to send lots on a regular basis.

He and I would go out for a meal after each sale and laugh at the foibles of the day. He was to be a big stepping-stone to my gathering sufficient knowledge to run better-quality sales, and one of the few people in the business that I could really trust. The best part was that he made everything fun and when together we laughed and giggled all day long about stupid things. John would do house clearances if there was anything antique in it and often found the odd badge in a drawer. He made a point of wearing these – just one at a time but they would usually have something a bit 'way out' impressed on them. A typical one had 'Butlins Darts Champion, 1964, Bognor Regis' impressed on it. I knew that he had never been to Butlins but if you challenged him on it you would get a whole load of nonsense back.

One day I acquired a similar sort of badge inscribed 'British Rabbit Council' so, after work, whilst waiting for John, I put it on to try and get even. Almost immediately the front door opened, and a man came in saying, "Evening Mr Lanham, I am from the Haver-hill Cavy and Coney Society and I was wondering if you would give us a donation as a prize in our show." Realising that I had no way of explaining my badge I immediately put the forefinger on my left hand over it and, with my thumb behind obscuring it completely, in some embarrassment I then benevolently said, "Of course I will", forgetting that I now needed my left hand to pull my wallet out of my left-side hip pocket. I was struggling with my right hand reaching across my back in a highly contorted manner when John quietly came in, noticing that I now had difficulty in opening up my wallet with the one hand and was forced to present the delighted cony and cavy man with the first note to come out – a 20. How John loved the spectacle and laughed himself silly as soon as the man departed.

We had expanded the estate agency with an office in Bury St Edmunds and another in Halesworth, before I realised that the estate agency was really not now for me. When I had entered the profession there had been a mutual respect for competitors, but with the advent of developers, escalating house prices and a winner-takes-all system, the respect of old seemed to have gone out of the window. Prosperity had brought its usual greed. What I mean is that if you went to take a property on, you could no longer tell the vendor the best price that you thought you might get for it, if you were allowed to take your time and could get good advertisements in the right monthly magazines etc. No, you knew that while you were spending the money on it and doing the work that can bring the optimum, it was highly likely that the vendor would become impatient and put the property in another agent's hands at a lower price. In other words there was little reward for doing your best. I had exhausted the thrill from winning in the estate agency. It was still highly remunerative financially, but my first love was in the cultural history that antique sales afforded, and I was feeling deprived of any flair that I might have whilst on the rostrum. Also I found that the young negotiators that I had got in did not have the same endeavour as myself and needed more supervision than I could give them. I had collected period items even whilst at school and I now wanted to get back to auctioneering and be away from the world of estate agency. I thought much about my dilemma and to let go all I had been through in building the firm up seemed stupid. I had met my friend John by then and whenever I was with him in the antiques everything was completely different. It was fun, which the estate agency no longer was. It was an enormous decision that weighed upon my health and when I told my doctor he advised me to go and see a private shrink in Cambridge. The only person that knew was my secretary. The lady shrink gave out no pills, all we did was sit and chat but it was a great help to me in making up my mind. Apparently I had fallen asleep in front of her on one early occasion, which told me something and helped in making what was to me a gigantic decision to turn my back on all that had made me who I was.

There was a Bury St Edmunds agent about this time who had given us a lot of gyp by spreading porkies behind our back – it all got reported back to me by a friendly antique dealer whose husband worked for the *Bury Free Press*. Having heard that we were closing our Bury office, knowing that we would not be able to handle it as we were closing, this agent sent us particulars of a property for us to sell on a half-share basis. I formed it into a dart and mounted it on a card saying, "Despatch to nearest wastepaper bin." I showed it to John, who said, "Neil, sometimes in this world you just have to express yourself." So I sent it to the culprit.

At the time that we opened our office in Bury St Edmunds, I arranged to announce ourselves by holding a Fine Art Sale at the prestigious Athenaeum Ballroom, which was situated on the Angel Hill. I would not say that it was a disaster, but I found it did not go as well as we hoped. This building was commodiously large, and I found that it was in fact too large. I felt that I could get a spark to fly across the floor of our little crowded saleroom in Clare, and large was not necessarily beautiful. Furthermore I found it amazing that the rival auctioneer who you will remember as I nicknamed him 'Beedme' turned up and wrote down in his catalogue what I assumed to be the buyers and prices just as another auctioneer had done at Cambridge

Machinery sales. Bob Grain would have put him right, I thought. How I would have loved to have said what he had.

I was not happy at all in finding that I was spending most of my time running from office to office covering up mistakes, and after much deliberation I chose to make the big decision that I thought would bring back my enthusiasm. But would it, I asked myself?

CHAPTER 9

Changes Afoot

I sold the lease of the Bury St Edmunds office to Charles Hawkins, the estate agents from King's Lynn. Michael Cross who had been a pupil with Horace Wilkin in King's Lynn was my best assistant. He was the one who was keen to open in his hometown of Halesworth, so I sold him that office even before it opened. He had been aware of our offset litho printing system and was to expand that side of the business to become Micropress, now a multinational printing company. The Haverhill goodwill and name of Chas Boardman and Son I sold to Christopher Blake, who moved the office down to the High Street. After only about six months or so on his own, January's, a Cambridge firm, took over. I was surprised as, for me, it had been a very remunerative business. As I came to expect, there were many rumours spread from people who did not understand why, but I felt relieved at leaving something that had taken some effort to build up. Former staff were asked many questions by onlookers. One, in his Haverhill accent, asked, "Has Nield had a nervous breakdown?" I got so fed up with it that come the spring I grew a full crop of tomatoes in both of my Haverhill office windows that had previously been full of photos of properties for sale – which brought another round of speculation. But I was just expressing myself as John put it!

I was now free from the estate agency but then it was still amazing how many estate agents attempted to sell fine art as a sort of part-time job. Fine objects did not sell themselves just by standing in the corner of a saleroom. They needed researching to find out exactly what they were, then marketing to find the most likely person wherever who would buy them. With the enormous help and belief that Rudyard Kipling had afforded me, I could now assemble his platoon of six honest serving men and take my beliefs out into the wild blue yonder.

Porters are an important part of the sale. Originally, Mr Boardman had Tom Morgan, his gardener, and Wingy Farrant, a lovely old boy who had lost an arm in the First World War and now kept a sweet-shop. He was as strong with his one arm as most people are with two. They were followed by Percy Sizer who had served in the South Africa Campaign and Ben Simonds, another gardener. I remember one of these porters being asked by a lady, "Is that item gold?" and the porters replying, "That is if it is not brass, ma'am" knowing full well that it was brass. Let's just say that they did their best. Then various other floaters came and went, until we acquired the full-time services of John Bartlett, a most capable man in every respect. He once changed the engine of one of the firm's cars, outside, under canvas. I remember at one Christmas party he sat at the table writing as everyone had got down from supper, then came through after about five minutes with a poem that was entitled 'The Rorty Auctioneer' and you can guess who that was about. I had been deemed to be at work at the office on Christmas Day.

He failed to arrive one day after he had not been there long and when I asked him what was wrong he just said "Benskins", who were brewers. He had enough about him to get away with anything. I did not care as long as I felt that he was totally on my side, or at least the firm's.

After Margaret had left Boardmans, she started a little antique shop, in Clare, that she called 'Granny's Attic'. She still worked for us on sale days, so she was asked to the Christmas party as ever. This year she produced a little present from Granny's Attic for everyone and for John Bartlett it was a chamber pot. We were at the Norney Moat House and after dinner everyone came back into the bar where there was no other customers, and John Bartlett insisted on buying drinks all round. Everyone ordered their favourite tipple with pride, that is until John lined the drinks all up along the bar, then tipped them one by one into his Christmas present, the chamber pot. He then passed this pale green liquid in its natural vessel round and everyone was expected to drink of it. I had to play my part, but some did not.

John brought his drinking friend Bill Jolly to help with the sales and he was an excellent worker. However, tales went around about his nocturnal habits. I did not believe them until I came back home one midday, where he worked from, to find a whole lot of long nets laid out on my lawn and Bill mending them. Now, nets come in all shapes and sizes but ones like this I knew were only for one purpose, and that is for trained dogs to drive pheasants into when they are sitting out on the stubble in early autumn. About this time I was going on holiday and I left John Bartlett, as caretaker, the key of our house. Before I went he asked if I would like a brace of pheasants. If so he would put them in my deep freeze. When I came home from holiday I found that our deep freeze was chock-a-block full, with no less than 40 or more pheasants. I knew that these had all come from land belonging to a gentleman who was a very good client of ours. So, imagining what it would be like if I was caught with these long tailed 'uns, I demanded that they got rid of them as soon as possible. Where they went I do not know but it did not take them long.

Fred Larter from Norwich came into the office one day saying that he was staying with his daughter in Haverhill and that he had worked as a porter, amongst other places, for Noel Abel, and that he knew how to show a piece to its best advantage. He came regularly after that, and it soon became apparent that he was as artful as they come. He was given a free catalogue for himself to use as part of his job, but within a few moments he had sold it and wanted another one. However, he fitted quite well into the drinking culture that was going on at that time. One time, for insurance purposes, he was going to be nightwatchman but, being suspicious, I went over to the saleroom and of course he was not there. I however managed to get the landlord's son from the pub next door to do it.

After a sale in Bury we all went to the beautiful old Cupola House for a drink. I noticed that Fred had a white-coloured drink, so I asked John Bartlett what it was. "Oh that's disco valente!" he said. "It's a new drink, would you like some, it has a rich peppermint taste."

"Yes I would like to try it," I said, and a few minutes later a glass was passed to me by the landlady, and they all wanted to know what I thought of it. Unbeknown to me, Fred had a bad stomach through drinking too much the night before, and this white peppermint drink was what the chemist had prescribed.

Fred, however, did get us some antiques from a lady in Norwich that he helped, but we did not see him for a long time after that. A member of the staff came across him when she stood next to him in a queue at Yarmouth races one day. She had a chat with him afterwards, to find that when he started talking about the old days at Boardmans, a tear rolled down his cheek.

John Bartlett went to look at a pantechnicon lorry for me that a local house removers had for sale. He then came back with a proposition that he wanted to buy it for himself, and would I lend him the money which I reluctantly did. The next thing was that he wanted a day off to do deliveries for people, and slowly we drifted apart until he left and later went to Cheffins, another auctioneer. Sadly John later died from prostate cancer. I had a letter from him some time before that, saying that nowhere had meant the same to him as Boardmans. I cannot think why, because I drove them all very hard, but as I said, they could do whatever they liked, as long as I felt that they were on my side. Yes, that was what was important to me and when they left, in a strange way, I felt that a part of me went with them.

Things slowly drifted along in the saleroom and we seemed to be taking a lot of dealer's lots from their own descriptions, and a lot of them were from the Ipswich area. Ipswich had been the cabinet-making centre of Great Britain and the company behind this had been Tibbenhams. Tibbenhams could and would reproduce anything. When Cescinsky and Gribble produced their two-volume book on oak and early furniture in the early twentieth century, Tibbenhams had produced a pricelist for the many pieces illustrated. An Ipswich lacquerer named Archibald became a legend in his own right, and it was said that he would lacquer one door with one hand and the other door with the other hand at the same time. Other firms followed on but what the individual cabinetmakers could do to make freshly made furniture look period was remarkable.

Referring back to Rudyard Kipling's saying about his six honest serving men being What, Where, Why, Who, How and When; this discovery was absolutely brilliant for cataloguing, because I realised that if I could answer these six things then I could fully catalogue any item that we were to sell. Why it is so important is that 'What' is immediately visible, but not necessarily the other five, and it made you bring the invisibles into focus. I later discovered that I could use the same criteria for finding the most likely buyer. I was amazed that I had not seen it quoted or used before, but although I had passed my chartered surveyor exams, I found very little instruction was given by them on the subject that I wished to follow, and I became suspicious of any so-called wisdom out of a book. Books were excellent for reference (the What) but the rest, I believe, can only come from prolonged experience.

I now wished to become more professional all round and had to decide how to take our antique sales forward. We had already received a backlash from locals when we stopped taking beds, cookers and modern furniture. I had felt that the general standard of the sale had increased following this. It had further been embarrassing at that time, when a dealer from away entered by post a bacon cupboard that turned out to be an oak wardrobe that John said looked as though it had been left for a month in a duck pond. So modern reproduction and fakes of any kind just had to go. 'Fakenham' was the word that I put on this faked furniture – from the town in Norfolk.

We had held several furniture and house contents sales at Haverhill Corn Exchange, but one day, due to the proximity of the residence we were emptying, decided to hold one at the Town Hall, Clare. I remember this sale quite well as our gardener/porter came up asking "Can you put this pocket watch in the sale for me as an extra lot?" On seeing the distinct digital Turkish numerals, "It's Turkish," I said. To which he replied, "I know." "How do you know that?" I asked. "Well," he said, "when we landed at Gallipoli the Turks kept us penned on the beach, picking us off for so long that, when we did reach the top of the cliff, the first Turk that I shot, I took his watch and this is it."

My first auction sale at Clare Town Hall went well, and afterwards we were approached by one of the buyers. He was well dressed in a dark blue mohair suit, and said that he could put a few lots in when we had another sale. Apart from John Tasker, on a special occasion, I had not imagined a dealer wanting to put lots into one of our general sales – it had never happened before. Anyway when the next sale came round, we contacted him, and he then sent a list of mainly silver that he wanted to sell. It all did extremely well. In the pub afterwards he told hilarious tales about shippers. "What are they?" I asked in innocence. "You mean you don't know what a shipper is?" he said, and then launched into a vivid description of how they are people who ship things abroad. This was something that I had not heard of at the time, and they certainly had not been seen at our sales. He went on to tell us how they all had their 'slaves' who sat in great big warehouses sorting out, and matching, the glass of four-bottle cruet sets, and also did the same with jug and basin sets in rows, as far as the eye could see. He even gave great descriptions of the alleged slaves which made me curl up with laughter. I found it difficult to take all this in, as, in my innocence, I knew nothing of it at all.

He then started on about Bermondsey weekly market. I had been to Petticoat Lane and seen the spivs in action, and their skill in 'getting an edge' when selling out of a suitcase had greatly appealed to me, as it was sort of similar to the skill of an auctioneer. He offered to take me to Bermondsey Market with him. I readily agreed to this. "OK," he said, "meet me at The Albert at Colchester at 5am and bring a pocket torch with you, and some cash." I drew £100 out of the bank and was in fact waiting at The Albert, when a herd of bullocks stormed past, with drovers following after. Up comes the dealer in his estate car with a big dent in the roof from when he had carried home from holiday a heavy marble figure. He had a few things in the back of his car, including a percussion blunderbuss for which I said, "How much do you want for that?" And I then spent £30 of my £100 on it.

It was dark when we arrived at the market, where loads of people were going round with their torches. I enquired about a bugle which was incomplete and the stallholder soon told me, "You've gotta take it to Lincoln's Inn and get it a moufepiece." I did not get it, but my new mate explained that a 'moufe'piece is cockney slang for a barrister (mouth-piece). I then bought what I thought was a Victorian cranberry glass sugar shaker which, as daylight slowly dawned, I realised was brand new and that the plain glass had been covered over with crimson nail varnish. Like the blunderbuss, I still have that too. It was all a reminder of what my Grandfather meant when he said, "Let your eye be your guide and your money the last thing that you part with." I was to learn several lessons that day.

I was however now out of the estate agency. Footloose and fancy free, and, in spite of my naivety, I was raring to go. The mohair-suited dealer then introduced me to his friend called Tick, who also told great tales of how he used to go to flea markets in Brussels. So after some consideration, Hazel, my wife-to-be, and I, decided to go and have a look. There seemed to be an underworld that I knew absolutely nothing of, and which I was determined to find out about. We took the Friday night sleeper boat from Harwich. I distinctly remember this, as on a poster that read 'Harwich for the continent' some graffiti wag had written 'and Dovercourt for the incontinent'.

We arrived early morning in The Hook of Holland and drove down through Antwerp, a very old city which still showed many scars of war, then on to Brussels, where we looked at a Saturday flea market near a church, then had a great Mexican meal in one of the many different international restaurants, the like of which we did not have in the UK. We stayed the night, then looked at the Sunday morning flea market, and came home to be at work for about 9.30. It was exciting. Hazel, who was a bit of a dabbler, loved it. We just bought anything that was different, from zip-up shoes to bellbottom trousers. It was great fun as well as an education.

John Tasker said that he was going on a buying trip up the north and suggested that I might have a day or two off. Tick was there at the time and said that he would like to come as well, so we took my Volvo Estate and ventured forth. I did not broadcast the fact that I was going on holiday with two antique dealers, for fear of more speculation, but I remember that we reached Harrogate and stayed at the Swan Hotel, where the landlady said that she had been an antique dealer and would show us some things that she wanted to sell the next morning. In her store the boys had a field day and bought so much that I had to go to a bank to get more cash for them. The only thing that I bought was an eighteenth-century red tortoiseshell and Mother-of-pearl table cabinet of six small drawers. I gave the good lady £250 for it, which I thought was a lot, and gave it to Hazel as a present when I got home. She said that she would like to keep her needlework things in it. About 30 years later I sold it for over £2,000. It had originated in Mexico and in all that time I had not known that.

The thing that I remember most about that trip was that when John told us a story of when he was doing his National Service in the Royal Airforce that the barber was the most popular chap on the camp and John had worked out his ploy. Apparently the camp barber, just as he was settling you into the chair would say to you, of the person vacating the chair, in a manner that they could just hear "What an interesting person he is" or words to that effect, so that they went out feeling ten feet tall. Tick could not forget it, and even if we went to a café, just as the waitress had turned to walk away, and so that she could hear, he would say, "What a nice girl" or something similar. I cringed but you could see the waitress become affected and positively purr.

The big provincial fine art auctioneers at this time were Henry Spencer and Son of Retford, Nottinghamshire, who were holding

John and Tick up north.

marquee sales on the premises up and down the East Coast of England and had a very high reputation. When they held a sale at Wixoe, which was very near to Clare, where we were holding our sales, I viewed the sale and got talking to one of their assistants, Alan Fitchett. As a result of this he came and joined our team. Rupert Spencer was the senior partner in his firm, and I had, with admiration, seen him in action. Part of his technique was to tell uplifting stories during the sale about what a lovely day it was, and how great was our magnificent country. Although the bidders laughed he raised the tempo and bonhomie, I am sure that the feeling of wellbeing that he created paid dividends. Alan smartened up our image a lot. We now put the catalogue out to print and he made sure that it was accurate and that items were not over-catalogued. We now called ourselves Fine Art Auctioneers, and this seemed to take us another step forward. We engaged the small local firm of E & E Plumridge, from nearby Linton, to print our catalogues and although things got very close from time to time they never let us down.

To get our catalogues out on time was indeed a challenging task because time was of the essence. At one end we had to put great pressure on vendors to bring their lots in time for proper research, cataloguing, and photographing, and at the other end the envelopes needed to be 'stuffed' quickly to get them to the post office to go out a fortnight before the sale to reach prospective purchasers across the world, including the USA, Japan and Chile. So stuffing day was an important one and for this we engaged all the itinerant staff we could. I remember a sixth-form boy on holiday from a major public school coming in to help. We put him in a room on his own to get on with putting the catalogues into envelopes. When we took him a cup of tea about two hours later we found that he had licked all the self-seal envelopes. He came to help several times after that but was never allowed to forget it. A lot of would-be auctioneers, who had a degree in Fine Art from Southampton University, came to help as they were finding difficulty in obtaining a position due to their lack of experience. "The only source of knowledge is experience," said Albert Einstein and was he ever right!

Alan Fitchett, however, was an excellent cataloguer and always looked the part in his velvet suits and flared sleeves that showed lace cuffs, but he did not stop with us long. It seems that our successes had brought him, as our Fine Art manager, recognition and he was soon offered a saleroom of his own to manage in Brighton. Alan told us tales of how the picture cataloguers at Henry Spencer's, when going in the car, would recognise the idiosyncrasies of various artists in the landscapes that they were passing and make a game of it. I liked the idea and felt that it showed a deep appreciation of the job that they were doing. I remember the evening that he came and told me that he wanted to leave. As I had come to expect with big events, I did not sleep that night thinking about it, but in tossing and turning I decided what I was going to do. I took back full control of the Fine Art department, and, with the help of John Tasker, who now came down every sale and stayed a day or two with my wife Hazel and I, we managed to get the cataloguing done, and somehow continued to expand. All my life I have had problems sleeping after a setback, but my subconscious mind has always come to my rescue and helped me decide by next morning what I should do.

We had acquired the services of a Mrs Swan to be Alan Fitchett's secretary and she was keen to stay on after he departed. She was an intelligent lady, an excellent secretary who could flare up and take umbrage very quickly by walking straight out. I persevered with her because I knew that she was always on our side, and she always did come back.

One day a set of Constable drawings arrived by carrier with instructions how we could fully catalogue them. With each of them came a label where they were exhibited at the turn of the century by a well-known London dealer. We duly advertised them and received enquiries, but before the sale one of Constable's relatives, who could not have possibly seen them, said on local radio that they were probably not right and most likely to be by his compatriot George Frost, which quite infuriated me as I had already suffered this attitude that any saleroom outside of London was incapable of handling such things and, besides, even if he had been an expert on his relative's drawings he simply had not seen them. It is a mere coincidence however that the drawings were not right as our research later revealed. They did not sell and, unbeknown to me, the vendor was furious with us for not cataloguing them as being right. Mrs Swan had gone walkabout when this happened but she wrote a letter asking if she could come back and that she had something to tell us. When she returned she revealed that the vendor had sent a private investigator to check me out – to no avail as she had given me a good reference. I still do not know why the vendor did this. Over the next year or two I watched as these same drawings came up for sale in other provincial salerooms. I thought for a long while as to what I should do and asked myself would I appreciate an auctioneer phoning me if the same thing had happened. Yes, I thought, and duly phoned the auctioneers and told them of our experiences. I similarly did the same when a painting that we sold had now acquired a signature that it did not have when we sold it.

I would not call it complete doldrums, but things had not been going too well in dear Old Blighty. President De Gaulle, in France, would not let us into the Common Market, and the Americans would not lend us any more money, when suddenly a buyer from Belgium arrived in the saleroom and bought about 25 lots of furniture. I had not experienced a buyer from abroad bidding in our sale before and at first thought it a bit of a random novelty, but after the sale I carefully noted which lots he had bought.

I had not realised the effect that it was going to have on us, but, as I said earlier, in 1967 Harold Wilson and his government devalued the pound by 14%. What this meant was that whilst we had to give no more money for British-made goods, £100 spent abroad brought only £86 of the prior value. Similarly, those people from the Continent who wished to buy British now had a 14% advantage. Of course we sent the next sale catalogue to our new buyer from Belgium and he came and again bought every lot of oak that we had. Carefully noting the lots the Belgium buyer bought, I told my friend John to get out and buy all the oak and early furniture that he could, and if he ran out of money then I would advance him what he needed against the goods. I had not acquired much wealth, but having realised the great opportunity that lay before us I was determined to use what little I had to the benefit of my business. Don't forget that I was fresh, young, innocent and raring to go in the way that I naively thought was right. I had no masters to hold me back and had little of the approved protocol. This was the 'cutting edge of change' and my peculiar situation had empowered me to realise it.

John was a regular buyer at one particular saleroom in his area where he had fallen out with the local dealers. They were spiteful, he explained, so he made sure that he always attended this saleroom and marked every lot within a bid or two of what he thought that he could get for it. John duly bought all the oak he could for our sale, phoned for an advance, then took the money after it had all sold to invest in more. It was then that I decided to hold a sale that was just restricted to oak, walnut and all early artefacts, and John said that he was going up the north again on one of his old runs to buy all he could. I, in turn, now advertised the sale where we thought the buyers were, this being in Belgian, Dutch and German magazines. And at the resulting sale we found that for most things the prices had doubled. For example, a standard nineteenth-century three-four drawer oak bureau which had been £250 pounds now made £500 all of the time. It was noticed that other auctioneers appeared to either not notice or recognise this new Continental market. John said that for a year after the hike in oak bureaux price you could still buy them in the north of England at the old price of £250. In a local Suffolk saleroom there had been a lot of 35 heavy oak schoolroom chairs. For the English trade they were late nineteenth century and being out of period had been sold for only £50 in total to sit in a second-hand furniture dealer's shop. They were then acquired to be put in our saleroom, where we divided them into three lots to make a staggering £3,000 in total. So £50 to £3,000 in the course of a few miles.

Nineteenth-century oak in this country, such as the chairs above, had been totally out of fashion and not wanted, but the new Continental trade knew nothing of this and they were all brought in to the newly arrived price level. Fine Georgian mahogany furniture was not part of the new hike in trade and just sat in dealers' shops, who it seems disliked it and were not able to understand the change and above all the reason behind it. On passing a Cambridge mahogany dealer's shop, where I knew the proprietor as he used to help us catalogue at Grain and Chalk, I popped in to say hello. In two minutes I became aware that I was not popular for what I had done to his trade. It just seemed to me that he was inflexible and unable to move with the changing times.

We had a phone call from a titled gentleman that I knew well, who was a member of a historic local family. On arrival he said, "I hear that you have someone buying for you on the Continent." This totally incorrect statement was the summary of all the claptrap that seemed to follow our success. It was no use thinking that it was unfair as nothing was further from the truth. One could not fight against it, but just ignore it. I just had an enormous appreciation of the job that I was now doing and I had always been like that. I have collected what I think are interesting things since my schooldays and my grand-Mother had given me her old dowry chest to put in the Staffordshire pot lids, figures and other old things from her childhood, and even old disused hand tools from the farm. I had traded with a boy at school an old unusable pin fire shotgun that I found in a wood and cleaned up. I had sort of been in my own business in trading and swopping stamps and unwanted Christmas presents since the cradle almost, and have keepsakes of everything from that age that bring back many happy memories as they all tell their own story. No, if I had not had the eye and love for things of timeless quality that carried our history, I would not be an auctioneer and would still have been doing the far more remunerative estate agency or copying ordnance plans in a lonely garret.

John, when in our area, would call in at local dealers and for the hell of it say that he was down to view Boardmans. Those that attended our sales were very supportive, but many it seems did not believe the prices that we reported locally and to the *Antique Trades Gazette*, which had now become the major trade weekly magazine. I ignored the tittle-tattle and just got on with the job. If we got it booked early enough we would take the double-page centre spread of the *Antique Trades Gazette*, and I have had dealers phone up with a good lot saying that they would only let us sell it on condition that a photograph of the item would be illustrated on this double-page centre spread. You have to speculate to accumulate.

The only other firm of auctioneers that I knew of that had recognised the new oak order was a firm called King and Chasemore from the south of England, and I believe that they were taken over by a leading firm of London auctioneers. I only ever spoke to their principal once in later years, and he said that he had always kept an eye on what we were up to, as we indeed had watched what they were doing. Locally I think that almost all other East Anglian auctioneers came into our saleroom for some reason or another looking as if they were going to discover the hen that was laying our golden eggs or something similar. Our Norfolk porter, Fred Larter, reported to me that he had seen Noel Able and others from his area, as well as Bob Arnold from Cambridge. A representative from Boardmans and Oliver of

Sudbury just stood open-mouthed as if he could not believe it. Most viewers in our oak sales just seemed to pick out a few lots but the dealer that I admired most came from the south coast of England and stayed overnight locally with his wife, and marked his catalogue with how much he could bid to on every single lot. Wise, I thought as he was the only one to do it, and even in the best of sales there will be pieces slip through that no one has thought about.

About this time, if I had anything brought in to me to sell and I did not know what it was, without saying who I was, I would take it up to the leading London auctioneers who always had an 'expert' on their front desk to give an opinion. One day I took up a little wall-mounted rack that I knew was made before the seventeenth century. It had a boarded back, four shaped partitions that I thought were maybe for Samurai swords. The person on the front desk dismissed it as nothing much. I later found out that it was a rack for various spits upon which anything from a lark upwards would be turned and cooked over an open fire and as such quite rare. On another occasion, I took up to the London auctioneers to get the value of an early seascape painting by Abraham Willaerts. We duly sold it, fully catalogued, but the purchaser brought it back saying that the same London saleroom had said that it was not painted by this artist. I phoned the vendor who said that it had been authenticated by Mr Archibald at the National Maritime Museum. I sent a photo to Mr Archibald, who wrote back saying that the painting in his opinion was by Willaerts. I sent him a donation towards his museum. Following these adventures I became less interested in what other auctioneers thought and was determined to be able to rely on myself – sink or swim.

It seemed standard for some would-be dealers to come out of the city thinking that they would get a bargain in the country, and if they found that they could not make a profit on the lot in question, would make whatever excuse they could to bring it back. If I thought that they had a case I would give them their money back as soon as

I could. But few, I found, had a legitimate reason. I did realise that most of the best things in the world were sold through the London salerooms, so I decided to take their catalogues of all furniture and certain painting sales. It was very costly, but it was the best factual reference for identification and an up-to-date price. I did not agree with getting help from so-called 'experts' as their opinion was not always based on fact; furthermore I found that as they did not have a vested interest they would not commit themselves to the firm opinion that was needed. Whereas I would, on my client's behalf, take that risk, if risk it be as the article would make considerably more when fully catalogued, with us having shown our full belief in it. I had a friend who had a drawing by a certain artist that was unsigned, so he took to the leading expert on that artist for an opinion. The 'expert' said that it was not right as in this period the artist only drew on pink paper which was not the case with this drawing. Having taken it home my friend decided to break the seal on the back and take the drawing out of its frame, whereupon he found that the paper that had been protected behind the mount was pink and the rest, where it was drawn upon, had faded to white. It seemed to me that the 'expert' knew about coloured paper but little else. Although there were a few people with great knowledge I found that most of them not having a vested interest would not put their neck on the line, so such opinions were valueless.

Having analysed and considered carefully what went on in the London salerooms, I realised that it was probable that they were not successful in securing a very high proportion of things that came within their reach. I then became determined that I should deal personally with everyone that approached us who may have an item for sale and that there would have to be good reason if we did not get the item. This was firstly on the telephone, particularly on the day after the sale. So as busy as I was, I would still grab the phone when someone enquired what a certain lot had realised. I developed a quick patter that engaged them in conversation, probably saying, "That was a good price, wasn't it?" And if they said, "Yes," then I would cheekily venture "Have you got one like it?" It was amazing how many people had phoned only because they had one like it. If they then sounded as if they might sell it, I became determined not to lose it. I remember a gentleman from Wales phoning up about the price of a clock that we had sold. We chatted and when I realised that he had some good things I was determined that he would sell them only through ourselves. I firstly offered him a better rate of commission than he had been paying in other salerooms, inclusive of the many extras that he had paid elsewhere by way of insurance and photography and even lotting-up charges. "But what about the cost of transport?" he said, "It's a very long way."

"Leave that to me," I said. "I'll stand that too if you are going to send me some good lots." I knew a transporter in Bournemouth who sent a big furniture van to Wales once a month, and the same to East Anglia, and that whilst this would take time and I had to pay for it, excellent business could be – and was – done, to great satisfaction all round. This gentleman had been the editor of one of the major antique magazines and although now in his old age had been an avid collector, and as such, was an ideal vendor.

Things seemed to be going fairly well and on a Monday night – it was the first of November 1976 – I was waiting in our office for John to arrive as usual for the Wednesday sale. Unlike myself he was always on time, but this time he was late. So I phoned his Mother who said that he had left on time. He still did not arrive so I phoned the police somewhere about where he might have been on the road. I eventually got through to a police sergeant, who asked if I was sitting down. Then he told me, "Your friend has just been killed in a motor accident. His van collided with a brick lorry." When such a thing suddenly happens your first reaction is disbelief, and I still cannot explain my anguish. I tried to pretend that I would not miss him, knowing that

I desperately would, and strangely wished that I had been with him so that I would have known what had happened. I very rarely cry but about a fortnight after it happened I uncontrollably broke down. I asked many questions in my mind, and even went to see his mangled van and also his mangled body, but no one could tell me how it had happened. He was my best friend and also many other people's best friend. I was one of six pallbearers at Harringworth Church near Uppingham, where he lies buried, but far from forgotten by those whose lives he touched. The fun-loving John could be most frivolous at times in pursuit of humour, yet he loved quality in everything. Unbeknown to myself and others that I knew, John had written poetry and even had articles published on

John Tasker.

Dylan Thomas. His Mother got his writings together and published them in a book and the last poem that he had written only a few days before his death was read at his funeral. It showed that he also had religion and I knew nothing of it. Anyway I had to get on with life despite this enormous shock and we had just received instructions that could bring us great success.

CHAPTER 10

The Winner is He Who
Can Go It Alone

The first big success we had at our little Clare Hall, that we would transpose into a saleroom on sale days, was that of a French boulle commode. This had belonged to a lady dealer from Newmarket, and a friend had told me that she was disappointed at the valuation she had been given for it by one of the major London auction houses. Apparently the auctioneers had been holding a local Open Day and I guess that they had sent the wrong person along to see it. One should realise that whilst they would undoubtedly have top experts in each field, there was probably only one or two experts in each department and most of them who would have only a general knowledge were as prone to making mistakes as much as anyone else. I gathered that they had verbally given her an opinion as to price of around £5,000, which to me was neither one thing nor the other, i.e., neither period nor reproduction.

I knew the lady well as she had been a regular at our sales, so when I next saw her I asked if I could go and see the piece, and she agreed. Now, it is almost certain that if you see a piece of boulle it will have been made circa 1900, and is a machine copy of the original handmade thing. I knew from my experience with early oak furniture the age of a piece by its construction, so I inspected the drawer linings first and to my surprise it confirmed that this was the real thing, made in the early 1700s, possibly by André-Charles Boulle himself, ebonist (cabinetmaker) to King Louis XIV of France. Reproduction boulle will be made in machine-cut brass marquetry and is almost everywhere. Although I had not handled a period piece of boulle, I knew what it was and had a good inclination of its rarity as this was indeed hand cut. For my own knowledge at that time, I used to take the catalogues of all the important furniture sales in England and the rest of Europe. It cost a lot of money to subscribe for this lot, but it is far better than taking an opinion from a dealer, who does not have a vested interest in the article, and you do not know how far you can trust them, and furthermore the dealer probably cannot keep their mouth shut.

I took a photograph, gave it to Pip, my typist, and told her to look through all of the Fine French Furniture catalogues of the previous five years. Pip came up with two similar commodes that had realised £12,000 each, another at £14,000, and one that had been sold at Mentmore for £20,000. Mentmore was the sale of the century almost. In normal circumstances I would not have repeated all these details to my vendor, as clients, whilst meaning well, can distort what you try to tell them and get overexcited, but in order to stand a chance of getting the piece I felt that we should tell her everything. I think from memory that we recommended a reserve of £15,000. I heard nothing more from our client, but heard from my informant that she had been to all the three major English auction houses and the highest that they had said, I am led to believe, was £15,000. One should not forget that this piece was out of condition and some of the brass marquetry was rising. However for auction purposes this showed its genuineness, and that it had not been tricked up for sale. I decided to phone her up and asked what she was going to do. She said that we could have it for sale, but the reserve was to be £20,000 – the same as the Mentmore one. I lost a night's sleep thinking how bad it would look if it did not sell, but fortune favours the brave it is said, so I phoned our client the next day to say that we would have a go.

One of the golden rules of this business is secrecy and it seems few can keep a secret – their ego will not allow it. So we made absolutely sure that no one other than myself and my secretary knew the reserve, including all the porters. Keeping mum is vital, and in those days an estimate was not expected, and we were determined not to give any indication. We duly advertised the item both in the UK and abroad. We had a lady called Lorna Noble who made Continental advertisements for us and she would save most of the important international magazines. We went through them all with a fine-tooth comb, sending complementary catalogues to everyone who had exhibited at Paris exhibitions and to everyone who we thought might have an interest. Before this sale we had never had even a black and white photograph printed within the catalogue but for this one we had made a separate wraparound cover with a colour photograph of the commode on the front. It was not high-quality, but I think that this added to the ambience in showing that it was a genuine sale.

There were enquiries from all over. It was well-viewed and one man took every escutcheon off to see the back of each plate, then put them back. I had arranged for it to be the last lot of the day and was still determined to keep my thoughts a secret. Viewers seemed to be suspicious of one another and several asked if a big, tall man with a ginger moustache had viewed the sale. I replied in the negative and told the porters to do the same. At last we got to the important lot and, not wanting to reveal what I was thinking, I asked for a bid from the floor saying, "You make the bid and I will take it." I then poured myself a glass of water while I waited.

"One thousand pounds, sir," came a bid from a young man who I knew was about third generation of a family of international dealers from Bond Street. Now, in my opinion a poor auctioneer, knowing that the reserve was £20,000 – old 'beedme' perhaps – would have said, "No, that is not enough" and started begging. Not me, this was exactly what I wanted because the next bid would be £2,000 and I would make it so quick that no one had the time to say, "One thousand, two hundred" or whatever and if they did I would have politely ignored them. This way I could get into a rhythm of £1,000 increments with each bid, so £3,000 would be the next bid, which is what happened, then £4,000 and so on, until it reached the reserve of £20,000. This without showing any emotion whatsoever of the fact that it was now 'in the market'.

Then – £21,000, and on to a world record price at that time of £32,000, sold to a Frenchman. It is difficult to believe that this was in an age when there were no mobile phones, but more extraordinarily

Our first world record. The French Boulle Commode circa 1700. We had no telephone in the saleroom but it still realised £32,000.

we had no landlines in the saleroom at all. There had apparently been Frenchmen running backwards and forwards during the bidding to the phone box outside in the street. I love the mental image of that, because this apparent primitiveness just shows that the whole occasion was as genuine as you can get, and it is my belief that this image helped excite the bidders to bid as much money for the commode as they did. Later, when the lady vendor came in and asked how much it had made and we told her, she said, "I knew it would" and then cleared off saying nothing further.

I sent next door to the Bell Hotel for a bottle or two of the sparkling stuff and porters, staff and everyone rejoiced in our phenomenal success. "It is a poor heart that does not rejoice," said Jim Nicholls, one of the porters. However, the matter was not over, for it was exceedingly difficult at this time to get an export order, and the commode had to be sent abroad with a trusted shipper to collect the proceeds in France on an 'irrevocable bill of sale'. I was told that the commode had been bought by 'The League of Free Frenchmen'. Further enquiries revealed that the commode had been purchased originally by our lady vendor from a cottage within the curtilage of a very large estate that was indeed local and important. I still find it uncanny where things come from and go round and around and that we should be chosen by old father chance to bring them out again. I kept thinking that John would have been so proud for us.

In reflecting on how well we had done, I credit how we all kept quiet about the reserve because if that had got out it could well have been a big turnoff in the mind. It is far better for potential buyers to think that we still have straw in our hair.

"If A is success in life then A = X + Y + Z. X = work, Y = play, Z = keeping your mouth shut," said Albert Einstein.

I was now receiving far more entries than I could handle, and thought hard how I could use my time better. I had thought seriously of getting our own saleroom but found such a place difficult to find.

In fact Hazel and I had been down to Bristol to look at an excellent existing saleroom, but decided against such a move away from the area where we had many ties. When Boardmans was small, with fewer staff in the estate agency, I had felt that we were at our most efficient, but we had gradually lost that as the personnel grew. I enjoyed being the person that our clients all spoke to, who catalogued and sold everything, and spoke to every purchaser, and I did not want to lose that efficiency. When we had upped the standard of our saleroom we did it by cutting out all the goods at the lower end and I thought that we can do that again.

What we had been doing was going on calls to see pieces in situ, then waiting to see if we had proposed enough money for the vendor to decide whether to give it to us to sell. I decided that I was not going on those calls unless we really had to. I did not have the time, so we asked people to bring their goods to us. If they were too large, then a photo would do.

I was just applying my new policy when we had a phone call from the bursar of a Cambridge college saying that they had an oak cupboard that they wanted to dispose of. They knew nothing about it other than that it was an old oak cupboard but out of principle I said that I would go. Cambridge colleges were high on my list of complacent places, as they were run by academics, who very often did not know what they had got, and this appeared to be the case here. You may think this statement strange and unfair, however a large proportion of the things that we got in for sale were because the vendor had no idea what they had got. I had the feeling that if they had known how good the item was we would not have received instructions to sell. In fact I can think of two occasions where things were actually withdrawn, presumably to be sent to a London saleroom once we had told them how good the item was.

On inspecting the cupboard my jaw dropped. I had never sold such as this before. I had only seen them in the reference books. I had been taking the catalogues of the leading London auction houses

The 17th-century North Holland oak four-door cupboard from a Cambridge college that sold for £33,000. A world record for a single piece of oak at auction.

and was aware that one like this had made what was thought to be the highest price at auction for a single piece of oak at £17,500. The piece in question was a seventeenth-century Dutch oak four-door cupboard, with six carved allegorical panels, but what made it important was its presence and history – its what, where, why, who, how and when. In the sixteenth and seventeenth centuries, Holland was a very rich nation. They had colonised the East Indies, bringing back herbs, silk etc. There was a desire to find out about artefacts and gain knowledge of this newly discovered world. Amsterdam merchants had become very rich with international trading, and collecting New World artefacts had become the object of their desire. In this show of wealth and knowledge, this particular piece of furniture had become the most important piece of furniture, in the most important room, of arguably the most important merchants of the time.

We duly advertised it far and wide and when the sale came around more foreign accents were heard than English in the Bell Hotel next door to the saleroom. Our cupboard was a bit more important than most others, not just because of its quality, but also because instead of having five caryatid figures interspacing the doors ours had six, the extra one being in the centre of the lower part. This made it particularly stand out.

The morning of the sale I had my breakfast, as usual, at the Old Bear and Crown near the saleroom, and to my surprise there was a large table of about a dozen London-based dealers at a table on the left of the door, most of whom, in their deep Italian voices, said, "Good morning, sir." In the middle of my breakfast one of the young dealers from Kent came in and shouted across the room "Who's gonna buy this tatty old cupboard then?" To which I replied, "There is a load of tatty old people want it," not thinking for a minute that the Italians would be bidding.

The cupboard I sold in the same way as I had done the French commode, allowing the asking price to drop low so that I could only take big increments of £1,000 a time. It was sold to an Italian dealer for £33,000, a world record, exceeding the London price for the previous one by almost double. I am not at liberty to explain all but I think that there was a bit of disagreement amongst the dealers. However that is their business and not mine to ask questions.

Now the flipside!

The day after our sale I looked in the paper, and Geraldine Norman, their art correspondent, had written a double column on the cupboard, together with a photograph (which we had sent her in anticipation a few days before), giving great praise for not just the price, but the way we had handled the sale. I appreciated this, as before when we had done well all that the local TV would say was "at a saleroom in Suffolk". I felt that if anyone had as much as coughed at either Sotheby's or Christie's it would get reported with their name to the fore. I wrote and asked why we could not be put on an equal footing when we were making world records, and they were furthermore within the TV company's own local Suffolk area. I just wanted an even playing field.

After that, the TV cameras attended almost every sale, so for each one I got the porters to put a smart red velvet cloth over the table at which I sat, and this had the firm's insignia 'Boardman' big and bold in our style of lemon yellow on black across the front and sides so that when the cameras panned on me the firm's name would have to be included.

I cherished what Geraldine Norman had said about us, but when I spoke to the vendor, the bursar of the Cambridge college who had given us permission to use the college name, oh dear there was a different and unappreciative story and, in spite of the extraordinary price the college had received, much criticism. It seemed that the do-gooder attitude of some of the alumni, not knowing the real circumstances and that it was sold by those who in my opinion were the best possible auctioneers for the job, had complained to the college. As I have often found in life, those of little knowledge of the circumstances often make the most noise. There was part of me emotionally vested in the way we had handled and achieved this extraordinary price. I had arrived at this point through many hours of sweat, toil and enthusiasm – in fact I had given my all for this bursar, and in the same way as I could not accept punishment for what I had not done at school, I had difficulty in accepting this unfounded criticism. If I had done this for the money I would have stayed in the many, many times more remunerative estate agency but as they say in Newmarket, "The best jockeys are always found in the stands."

I reacted to all of this by spending almost the whole of my commission with a Dutch book dealer that had advertised in a major overseas magazine that we advertised in, by buying a copy of every book old or new on Dutch, Scandinavian, Flemish, Italian, German and French period furniture, several of which cost us over £100 each. They were to prove well worth it.

I knew, from my limited experience, that it is no good advertising unless you have something to advertise – something that will catch the eye, so we made the most of the occasion. The portrait-shape of the photograph made it very suitable for a single column advertisement, which I could stamp 'World record' over the top, and £33,000 underneath, keeping the cost to a minimum, and we ran it everywhere we could, for it is said that, "He who whispers down a well, about the goods he has to sell, will not make half as many dollars, as he who climbs a tree and hollers."

Later, when a friend asked me how we had made such an extraordinary price in seemingly backwoods circumstances, I thought and then replied, "Firstly by observing then thinking, questioning, and then believing that the answer was within our reach," and I arrogantly meant it, but somehow I felt that I could not tell him all that I really thought, because he would not understand and I would only dig myself in deeper into a quagmire as I had done before. My personal beliefs however were that I seemed to have developed a way of seeing things not just in the visible literal that is apparent to all but in the invisible principle of understanding that lay beyond and that this is best outlined in Kipling's saying.

The principle of understanding is something that will occur and occur again, so it is this that we should follow, and not the literal but understanding it does indeed take some thought. Thinking back, if I can be allowed to stand outside my arrogant self, I felt that I had acquired a new mantle and I wore it and I loved it. I saw myself not just as 'the auctioneer' but 'the marketeer' as well. I realised that my biggest contact with the antique-loving populous was through story, and that people believed this more if the press said it than if I said it. When one is cataloguing one is in fact telling factual stories from history, and I now used Rudyard Kipling's saying about his six honest serving men in everything that I did. I looked at every lot with a different percep-tion asking, "What is the story with this piece?" or "Could I make an interesting story about it, for everything has a story if only we can see it?" and I was determined to make those stories into a 'hook'. For those who do not know this word 'hook', it is the moment when if one were selling out of a suitcase in Oxford Street, for example, the onlooker is converted by the patter of the seller to become a desirous buyer. This was now going to be an important part of my job.

I discovered that most of what goes into the national press and TV comes from news agencies so I would phone them personally before a sale and send photographs, and a story that I had put together that lay behind my now 'highly interesting' lots. I would also prepare bulletins of prices and include photographs as alerts.

I would also advertise in glossy magazines prices realised. These were sent immediately after the lot was sold or, if very important, I would phone them immediately after the sale, as yesterday's news to them is valueless. I even went on a storytelling course only to find that my mum already did what they were trying to teach, only she did it naturally – the old natural way of passing meaning and with it wisdom.

I also tried to find the provenance of everything and how it was tied into history or people. Instead of just calling the item "a late-sixteenth-century such and such..." I would call it "An Elizabethan so and so..." I remember cataloguing an item that had come from a descendant of the Catesby family, who was an associate of Guy Fawkes, so we went to town on that. It all went together to help the price.

If an item could be tied to a particular place, I would send a presale report to the local regional paper. Or if I could find a house name on the title of a painting, for example, I would send a catalogue addressed to the occupier. It was surprising how many of those targeted would bid, as well as thank us for our ingenuity, as they would not have known otherwise. All this for free, whilst other auctioneers were noted as refusing to send their self-esteemed glossy catalogues out without prepayment. Could they not see that it was the goods that they were selling not their self-ego-boosting catalogues?

I attended all the major antique fairs and introduced myself around, and on occasion had a stand myself in order to meet as many potential buyers and sellers as possible. If I was sending our van to collect from a particular area and I knew other good vendors in that area, I phoned to tell them that if they had anything suitable I could collect it free of charge. I found it remarkable how many good sale items that the top dealers had in stock and were prepared to move on. These lots had simply become blighted for no reason. My friend John Tasker told me of a dealer he knew who used to trade by swopping items that stick – items that had been sitting in a shop for some time and no one had any idea why. He could apparently sniff out the stickers which the seller had become absolutely fed up with, then ask for the trade price, then the very best price, then he would ask if they would swop it for something in his van. He would then go along a street of antique dealers swopping all the way, and accumulating more value at each swop.

This may seem a bit far-fetched, but I can see it happening, as I have observed in the minimarket forces of the auction room how you are likely to have about ten would-be bidders for one or two lots, yet only two bidders for another lot, and then some lots no one at all has thought of buying. Such are the random laws of sales by market overt, and it is what keeps dealers going. I remember a very moderate sale, but one piece made an extraordinarily high sum which produced people coming up and saying what a wonderful sale I'd had. I also remember having for sale a fine Georgian press cupboard with an architectural pediment that did not sell as one had appeared in another auction almost exactly like ours and I think that people thought that ours was the same one. If I had my time again I would study the effect of randomness in auction prices and try to follow them through their up and down life in market forces.

Probably one of my best advertisements was when we produced a calendar of the previous year's sales. Having sorted photos of lots that had achieved our 12 best prices – one for each month of the year – we then displayed each sheet with a staggering price along the bottom and with the days of the month either side, and on a spare sheet at the back a little report on the year's trends. We sent one free of charge to every dealer in this country. It was an investment that produced business manyfold. The next best thing was when we produced our first catalogue by the new digital image. We were the first to do it and I announced our forwardness by placing a seemingly personal letter in each catalogue with an apology for the quality and asking people to bear with us whilst we experimented with this new digital age. How people love an apology, for it drew attention to the fact that our competitors had not yet arrived in the new age.

It took a long while for the wound that the bursar had made to heal following our extraordinary sale price of the Cambridge cupboard and their unappreciative comments, but I had to pick myself up and get ready to go again, which I soon did in reply to the umpteen people who now said that they had one of these cupboards.

It is extraordinary how a price like this blows away a lot of cobwebs. From out of almost every corner came cupboards for sale. One in the next sale came out of a coal shed, where it had laid completely unappreciated for many years. Whilst our cupboard was special, the normal price for a plainer example had been around £3,000–5,000. When we told the vendors of the coal hole cupboard this amount, they were not happy as they now wanted what the record one had made. After much cajoling, they agreed to accept a minimum of £5,000. The reserve was set at this, but we only just managed to get to it after running one sole bidder from about £2,000. I was relieved to get it gone, but the vendor's family then sent a letter of abuse, criticising everything about the sale that they could, including the way that I conducted it from the rostrum – I had never had that before. Why did they want so much and become so abusive and why was the extraordinary price of the Cambridge one so unappreciated? It was the philosopher Hume who said, "Passions rather than reason govern human behaviour" or as they say in Yorkshire, "There's now't as queer as folk."

We did get in some good cupboards though. One, a Cologne cupboard, went straight from us to a museum in Cologne at £3,000. It seems that every area in Holland, Germany and France had its own particular shrank or cupboard. With the knowledge I had obtained I was able to write an article for *The Antique Collector*, a leading magazine, showing over 20 examples and the areas that they were from, such as Amersland, Geldersland, Namur, Arnhem, Liege, Hamburg, Frankfurt, Cologne and Brugge, with carved scenes on the door after their artist Hans Memling. This last one sticks in my mind as one panel after Memling was of a man being flayed – skinned alive.

Cupboards galore of all sorts were now coming in. Since the extraordinary price of the first one, it seemed that everyone now thought that they had one and wanted me to inspect it. I travelled miles to see things that were nothing like what we had sold at all. I began to get irate with a lot of running around for nothing.

But I remember a man from Hadleigh in Mid Suffolk saying he had one in a basement of a Felixstowe hotel. Would I go and see it? I had to meet him in Hadleigh, and then follow him down to Felixstowe. I was now getting more and more irate as it seemed like I was on another wild goose chase, and I was getting worse the nearer that we got to Felixstowe. When we got there, I went downstairs to see what I was determined would be an abortion... there it was, a real good period cupboard that we sold for almost £7,000. So you never really know what you are going to get. My rule was whatever they said they had got probably was not what in truth correct, but there were bound to be other things in the house that made the journey worthwhile, so go as quick as you can.

On another occasion, a lady from Hurstpierpoint, right down on the south coast of England, phoned saying that she had an Arnhem cupboard. When she sent a photo I told her that it was a copy, probably made in the nineteenth century, and not of the period. After she had phoned about three more times stating that it had been seen by some knowledgeable person, and absolutely insisting that it was without doubt of the period, I said that I would go down in our lorry and collect it. I duly arranged for one of our staff to come with me on a certain Saturday to drive the van down with me to see it and collect it. On arriving and finding the house, I entered, only to find that it was as I first thought, a nineteenth-century copy. I was drained. It had taken us about four hours to get there, through the Dartford tunnel, and now four hours back. I think she knew all along that it was not old. Did she think that bringing it to me would somehow make it old? With this, and the lack of appreciation by the Cambridge college vendor, then abuse from the coal hole vendor, I began to think that the job was more about understanding the thinking of people than what their objects could bring and that is not far out.

But the oak spinoff was enormous and money trickled down so that antique shops were now springing up almost everywhere around us.

CHAPTER 11

Taking Stock

The night after a sale, my good wife not objecting, I would take the sale book up to bed with me and dictate, on a portable dictation machine, how we had done and all that had happened, while it was still fresh in my mind. I asked myself, regarding all the important lots, who bought it, and why, and asked then could it have made more? I also asked why a lot had not sold – sort of applying Kipling's honest serving men again. Gosh that Kipling is everywhere – he is not just a maker of luscious cakes. More important than Mr Kipling's cakes, I looked at all we had done and asked the question could it have been better? This included information about the porters, the bidding clerk, the photos, where the item had stood in the hall, what was the prior lot, and everything in the catalogue.

I found that there was so much psychology attached to the price achieved – one often has to stand outside themselves to envisage this. When selling, one only has about 30 seconds on each lot, so you have to use it well, and keeping the full attention of the public at all times is a large part of the success. To do this, I would sit as close to the potential bidders as possible so as to maintain order and keep the attention only on me. I would only read the lot number out and not the full description as they already knew that from the catalogue. And definitely not say words to the effect of "Isn't it lovely?" This I felt was so important, so as not to lose momentum, that I would even try to read the next lot out whilst still writing down details of the previous purchaser. All this to avoid the public starting to natter, and me losing the momentum, optimal attention and price. I would get the porters to hold all items up if possible, and definitely not take a lot down until all bidding had ended, because if they took it down before, it gave the impression that the bidding was over. I would never use a microphone, as people would not pay total attention to me, the conductor of the orchestra with the velvet glove extracting their money.

We kept a list of regular buyers, who always received free catalogues, but in addition we kept a specialist list upon which we added anyone anywhere who had advertised for, or who dealt in, certain particular items. We did not wait for them to come to us, and this was appreciated as it appeared that a lot of our competitors would not send a catalogue without payment and many times we were congratulated for doing this.

I often felt that the pomposity of auctioneers' catalogues in making everything sound marvellous needed bringing down a peg or two, so I decided that, just as a good after-dinner speaker will tell the first joke against himself so that he can then go on to insult others, I would do something similar in our catalogues. I decided to bring a little humour into the occasion. My friend Terry Challis the cartoonist for the *Watford Observer* invented 'Eric the Porter' and made humorous cartoons out of his eccentric events, most of which had actually happened in our auction. Eric had been discovered whilst he was looking in cuckoo clocks to try and find eggs!

Porters are important. Before the sale I would give a team talk and walk the saleroom with those who were going to show items, and remind them that good porters make a good auctioneer, in that as soon as I have called the lot number out they shout "Shown here" immediately, and that they should be well prepared in advance. I would tell them as little as possible before a sale for fear of being betrayed, but after the sale, when I took them all for a meal, we would rejoice and relax and they could ask me anything they liked as, in spite of my strict discipline, I wanted them to feel that they also had a part to play. On these occasions I would pay for the meal and they would pay for the drinks out of their tips. It worked well.

One should be very careful not to tell them much before the sale as I have heard that in a certain saleroom they were in the dealer's pay, so they could find out where the goods had come from. At viewing time they were told to be on parade like they were in the army and not to tell anyone anything, and that they should refer prospective purchasers to me for anything they wanted to know. I have seen prospective bidders on view day tell the porter that something is not quite correct with the lot, whether that was true or not, and you can bet that the porter will pass on that information to the next viewer – they cannot help themselves, their ego demands it.

Another discipline that I have seen go wrong is when porters hand one lot out of a cabinet to a viewer, then another lot to another viewer, then another, and then not get them all returned, and on the count-up leading to the sale day a lot is missing and we have been tricked. In the days before credit cards, we were let down a few times. Porters delivering to cars were asked to discreetly write on the pass that they retained the car number of the vehicle that they were delivering to. Then to keep mum and hand the receipt ticket to the office. Of course they could not keep it a secret and purchasers were known to say that they were not coming again because the porter had told them what I had requested. They should have been working for the firm, but in effect they were working for someone else – or themselves.

As I have already said, the catalogue is a legal document and one should say all you can to the advantage of the lot and declare nothing to its disadvantage unless legally obliged to. You should catalogue for your client who pays you, and not for yourself. Do not use meaningless words like 'lovely', 'beautiful' etc., whether the item is or not. That is for the purchaser to decide, not you, and it helps the ego of the purchaser in his 'discovery'. I suppose it is a bit like writing a book in that one should 'show' and let their opinion come from within and not 'tell' which they may reject.

In the saleroom there are places where items never seem to sell well. It is just the same in the catalogue. A poor price will invariably follow the Lord Mayor's show lot, because minds are disturbed and they are not concentrating. Try and get interesting things in your catalogue, even if they are not valuable, as they will bring people to the sale. Make your catalogue a psychological undersell that quietly implies that the room brims with interesting and as yet unexploited goodies awaiting a buyer's discovery. Never over-catalogue. When goods are offered in the country, the populous will expect you to be a bit naive so do not let them down and 'play the part', for it is wrong to be over-clever. I remember, before I knew better, calling an Italian chest of drawers by its 'book' name 'cassettone'. I can still picture the Italian dealers laughing when the lot came up. I did not do it again. Similarly we were in the country, and I believed that it is wrong for a seventeenth-century chair to be called anything as academic as a 'back stool'. I remember apologising to a very knowledgeable academic for it. He could call it what he liked in his published books – I nevertheless felt that this was right for us, the seemingly hick country people.

At house visits it is essential that you go straight away – waiting is a sin – then look everywhere because, what they think is valuable is mostly not – that goes to the crux of the matter. But there will be, for certain, other things that are valuable. Complacency rules and if there is one thing in this book that is important, this is it. I cannot emphasise this more strongly. I have been to a house where the best lot has been on the bonfire in the garden and have missed another very good lot for not going down into the unlit cellar. One day we sold a small sixteenth-century oak clinker-built ark. It had formerly had tools in it in an outside shed, and it had been missed by the representative of a big Midlands auctioneering firm. Repeat, missed by the big man. It had been noticed by the man who brought it to us on the house clearance man's van, and we gave him £100 for it. I believe from memory we made around £5,000 for the item and it now resides in the Shakespeare Memorial Museum in Stratford-upon-Avon, along with another piece that came from us. This was a sixteenth-century oak bench with pierced Gothic side rails, which although originating in Suffolk, had been sold to a buyer from Scotland. He did not like its blond colour so had covered it in an undesirable and almost unmovable wax, to the effect that it was now catalogued by a major auctioneer without a period. Yes! With no period at all by the allegedly top people.

So look everywhere, admit what you don't know, and be prepared to go away and find out the answer. By this I mean recognise when you do not know about an article and come home and take a reference before opening your mouth, for no man can be expected to know everything. I remember explaining to a client that I needed to go back to the office to do some research, only for them to tell me later "because you did not know what it was". What do you need to do to convince them, I ask?

We used to receive instructions from solicitors in a certain area to go and meet an executor who would then show us round the lots of a deceased estate to be sold. One might notice for example a fine Georgian Mahogany Halifax Longcase clock in the hall on the way in but the executor would in all probability want to start in the kitchen and follow on round the rest of the house first. As so often happened, you would take a load of old toot that you did not really want as you 'knew' that you were going to get the handsome clock, which you would do well with. But, when you got to the clock and started writing down details, the executor would invariably say "Oh no you cannot have the clock, the doctor admired it so much whenever he came and she so wanted him to have it so you cannot take that." I was to find that this damned doctor had his wretched name on all of the best pieces in his area. The worst thing was that I knew him socially and had even sold some of his gains for him. The worst bit was that he was good company and a very jovial fellow and I had been at a dinner party where he had relaxed and told us that a previous doctor for whom he had worked had told him: "The time to prescribe medicine is the time that the patient is just about to get better" – and I thought at the time that this summed him up a bit.

At a Sunday morning drinkies, where I had probably imbibed in too much Pommery's sparkling white, I was relaxed and, forgetting my 'Keep mum at all times' principle, related this story without mentioning the doctor by name. My listener of course would go and recognise who I was talking about and unbeknown to me the very doctor was in the next room. Whilst partaking another sip of Pommery's bubbly through the bottom of the glass I recognised someone approaching me very fast with long strides. It was none other than the doctor – the victim of my very story – saying, "Neil, I understand that you have been telling tales about me that are not true." I could not deny it, but I had rehearsed being caught out on occasions like this and did the only thing possible which was to immediately fall about laughing as loud and as long as I could and falling on him, in so doing, getting him to laugh as well. I had learned this ploy from my old mate John and recently given it the name of 'my Farage ploy' as that is what the politician seems to do when presented with a difficult question – a great technique. It worked, for the doctor now said, "well there was one lady that …", and then, "and another …", "and an old gentleman that had a Chippendale …." In fact, he admitted to far more than I knew about and could not stop talking about his acquisitions. Good stuff that Pommery's.

It was Dr Johnson who said that knowledge comes in two kinds: "That which you know and that which you know where to find." For me knowledge comes in three kinds: "That which you know, that which you know where to find and thirdly, and most importantly, that which you have not discovered yet." This may sound strange but try to recognise that there are things that I have not learned about yet. We are told that great philosophers have said that nothing exists unless you have experienced it, and I can well believe that, for I have found that it is so difficult to rationally convince people against their emotions. Facts must come before emotions if it is success that we are seeking.

Lastly, one should be bold and catalogue for your client. What I mean is if you think that the piece is right then stick your neck out and say so, for the lot will make more if your confidence in it is shown. How else can you show your undisputed belief? There is too much under-cataloguing and playing safe for one's self that lets your vendor down by playing into the buyer's hands. Private buyers particularly need the strength and certainty of your solid verification. In Newmarket they say, "I know you think that you can ride, but can you ride bold?" Well, you have to catalogue 'bold'. In fact be bold, competent, honest and true in all matters. The slogan of the Central Association of Agricultural Valuers, of whom I was a member of the Suffolk branch for 50 years, is "Do what is right, come what may." Some people may resent you doing that, but it is not a bad slogan to follow. Be honest and true to yourself and you will sleep better.

CHAPTER 12

A Great Day Out

I had a phone call one day from our best buyer of oak, who incidentally came from Belgium, asking if my wife and I would like to go and have lunch with him. On saying, "Yes, thank you, we would," he then said, "My plane will come and collect you from Cambridge airport at such and such a time." We duly arrived at the Belgian airport to find that the dealer had come to meet us in his vintage Rolls-Royce, taking us to one of those superb, small, fine-quality restaurants that they only seem to have in Belgium, before showing us around his fantastic stock. He had bought a seventeenth-century English oak refectory table from an Amsterdam saleroom of one of the major English auctioneers and wanted to put it in our saleroom, where he thought that he could get a good profit. He was right of course, but I cannot remember the exact price, although I think that he said that he had paid around £6,000 for it and wanted to send it to us. The table was long and had six turned legs and all-round stretchers, in a manner that suggested that it was from the first quarter of the seventeenth century. I had seen none better, for it had clearly never been in the hands of the self-styled 'restorer'. It duly arrived for auction and we sold it to a good English oak dealer for £20,000. What surprised me was that not one person knew that it had come straight out of a sale of one of the major British auctioneers. What a difference in price we made – why had they not had enough guile to have informed a few good English dealers, I asked myself.

Similarly, we achieved the same success a few years later for an Elizabethan oak draw leaf table that had been bought in USA for even less. Apparently the sale in USA had been advertised in this country, but few it seemed would take a chance on the table without inspecting it first. We had advertised it for sale in the *Yorkshire Post*, a regional paper with a good following of their weekly page advertising auction sales. We duly sold it to a private buyer from Yorkshire for £20,000.

The retired editor of our local paper phoned one day and said that in his neighbourhood rectory in Cambridgeshire there was a refectory table that they were selling for £400 and that I could go and look at it if I wanted to. "Is it for sale?" I asked. "Yes," he replied, "they have had someone out from a museum who says that it is an eighteenth-century elm farmhouse table and the best offer to date is £400. That is the price that they are going to take for it." So, in spite of getting into competition with all the others, I said that I would go and see it.

When I saw it, well you could have heard my jaw hit my chest in Moscow. It was not elm, it was early English walnut about eight feet long and it had had about everything under the sun happen to it, including umpteen coats of paint, mostly now worn through, later iron straps to the centre, and a curious mark of a crown over an elongated 'H' that I had never seen before. I knew immediately though what it was and asked where it had come from. "Thorney," came the reply. "That's it," I thought to myself. "It is early English and could be fourteenth or fifteenth century and certainly no later than early sixteenth-century English walnut, with the mark of Henry VIII at the dissolution of the monasteries." Henry VIII's men had destroyed 'popery', but what would be the point of destroying a good dining table? My colleague wanted me to put an offer in for it and kept saying anything over £400 would buy it. "No," I said, "I am a chartered surveyor, and you have come to me for advice. I cannot under those circumstances try to buy it." If it had been in the open market then that would have been a different story. "I think that it should be put into our next sale," I said.

I waited while the Church authorities decided and upon their approval I sent to have it collected. They asked for a reserve of only £400 on it, which in hindsight was ludicrously low, and it should have been better protected, but I did not know how to tell our vendors that they, in my opinion, had received erroneous advice from the local museum. The table did make several thousand and I am told that it now resides in a museum in Boston, USA.

On a similar principle, a dealer who was a runner (took things around to sell for other dealers) brought an item to me which he wanted to be sold in our next sale. On looking in the back of his van I saw another piece – a seventeenth-century cupboard that he wanted only £400 for, and I knew that it would do well in our sale. The cupboard was of an unusual Dutch type that has three cushion-raised panels to each of its two doors. I had seen similar but only in a book. I was excited and begged the runner to put it in the sale, but to no

The early 17th-century oak table bought in Amsterdam for £6,000 and sold by ourselves for £20,000.

avail. Despite begging and begging he would not budge, saying that anyone who offered £400 could have it. So I then arranged for a third party to buy it and enter it in our next sale. We duly advertised it with a photograph in a Continental magazine. My thoughts about its importance were confirmed when a man came from Belgium especially to buy it, bidding only on this one lot and paid the goodly sum of £2,000. I wished afterwards that I had never had anything to do with selling it before the auction, because it seemed that I had insulted the dealer who was running the article. After all, he was the dealer, and I never saw him again. Ego is a strange thing and takes a lot of forethought to understand.

Regarding refectory tables, another one that we sold for a record price at the time was not very old at all, and it had no need to pretend to be, for it had been made by the highly esteemed 'Mouseman', Robert Thompson of Kilburn, Yorkshire, who signed all his pieces with a mouse carved on it somewhere. It made £15,000 and now resides in the USA having obtained an animal import licence for the mouse – I joke of course, but that is the sort of question, I feel, that one might expect from the form-fillers at the customs!

I had a letter one day from the estate manager of Greene King, the brewers, to the effect that they wanted me to inspect and report on a six-leg oak refectory table at their public house at Ickleford in Hertfordshire. When I arrived the locals were playing dominoes at the table so I had to wait for closing time. During this wait, at least three of the locals came up to me individually and said words to the effect that they supposed that I was going to get it restored. "No I don't think so," I quietly replied, for I had long since inwardly objected to the use of the word 'restored'. I recalled an old cabinetmaker telling me that there is only one man that can make old and that's Jesus Christ, not me or you, so why use that word? Why did these people automatically think that it needed to go to a 'restorer' I asked myself, as my preliminary inspection revealed that there was nothing whatsoever wrong with it.

It seemed that this table had stood in this public house since time immemorial, because a window frame would have to be taken out for us to remove it. The highwayman Dick Turpin was reputed to have hidden under it and in the nineteenth century it had been in use to help the ladies of the village do their washing, and at another time it had been a part of the furniture when the room was in use as a court-house. It was even thought that a hostelry on this site could have been a dormitory for those who were building the church next door.

When the imbibers had dispersed, I had a good look at the table and found it to be as beautiful as only good period oak can be. What I mean by this is that oak has qualities that most other woods do not have. Of course quercus robur, as the academics call it, is strong and tough, but much more important than this, it has tannin in its veins and grains. What tannin does is, and this is very important, in a gentle heat, it oozes out of the grain very, very slowly over two, or three, or even four hundred years, filling it up and giving each piece a deep bluish-black all-over skin. It is not however as straightforward as that, as this tannin tends to get graduated, according to where the piece

has stood, the atmosphere and its general use and how it is dusted, into gradually wearing through this blackish skin to give a grad-uation of a beautiful rainbow of soft colours and a crusty texture. This colour, and you will have to look closely, runs from a deep dark bluish black, and even a greeny hue, gradually fading into a crimson red, into oranges and yellows, interspaced by the blackish tannin still in the grain. Then, where there are minute

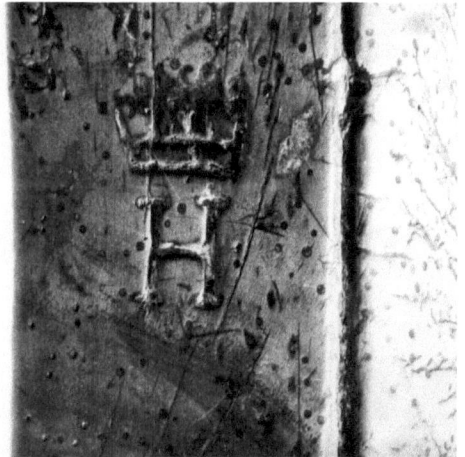

The mark of Henry VIII on the English walnut table.

165

crevasses caused by occasional misuse, this will be left with the natural tannin colour again or even specks of greyish white of congealed dust.

The old cabinetmaker was right, in that no mortal can make or fake it. I suppose it is because it is such an acquired appreciation that those without sufficient love and deep involvement with the whole concept of variation in colour seem unable to recognise it. People such as the 'experts' that said that our 1380 church pews were circa 1880 – you will come across these people soon, as you read this book, so be well armed. You may think that I am waxing too lyrical, but I could not believe it if I had not seen this effect go unrecognised by some senior museum curators and some senior antique valuers. It comes back to the wisdom of old Einstein again and his saying that "All knowledge comes from experience." I do not like constantly running down my competitors, but I find that I cannot get sufficient measurement on this big principle without doing so. I bear them absolutely no malice, but our little business relied upon a hands-on knowledge, as that was the only way that we could beat the big boys and earn ourselves an honest crust!

The other thing affecting the colour of oak is that if the piece has rested in a damp atmosphere, such as a church, then the tannin does not move and the piece in the damp atmosphere can acquire a distinctive whitish blond colour. As I write this I have next to me a nineteenth-century stool often described as a lacemaker's stool. It has an oval top in elm with pierced central hand-carrying hole and four-square section, slightly tapering legs in oak united by an all-around stretcher. What makes it beautiful in my eyes is that it has never been in the hands of that dreadful man who has to colour his work by going around with a French polish rag in his hand. It is not difficult to recognise his work, as the grain is not usually full, and it usually has a boring all-over single colour applied by colouring and applying a French polish type lacquer finish. Taking measurement from him, my stool is virginally beautiful. The only thing different from my description above is that my elm stool is pale in places where some idiot has spilt coffee over it – I wonder who that was. The naturally acquired skin on an old piece, as described above, will be that it is as smooth as a baby's bottom where the good housewife has weekly waxed it, usually with a concoction that has a high concentration of beeswax, forming an all-over skin that goes hard and shines when it is regularly polished. Its glass-like finish, when matured like this, gives a pleasurable touch. I have seen this tannin or similar come out of elm and walnut to lesser effect, but I have also seen its effect when coming out of ash, which, when cut at an angle into oysters has the most pleasing effect.

I used to be a member of the Furniture History Society and when they held their annual two-day meeting in Cambridge I went along. We met at Trinity College library where it was explained that the kind of almost knotless oak was from Scandinavia and would have been brought from King's Lynn docks by lighters (river craft) along the rivers Ouse and Cam, to the backs in Cambridge. King's College chapel which is older still was most certainly constructed the same way and the darkness of its colour is almost certainly caused by tannin. I remember having an oak refectory table that came from one of these colleges which was of the earliest design, with three cruciform supporting pedestals. Over about five centuries it had been restored and restored, no doubt by the college joiners until there was almost nothing left of the original. King's College is a most interesting place to go. They have in their records the names of the Italian artisans who first worked upon it in 1446. The sheer sides of the chapel walls are a tribute to those men.

At an early stage in this venture, Hazel and I went on holiday to Dublin and being 'ever so clever' I bought a refectory table. It was a fake and I was the 'know all' who dropped us in it. The next one I bought, to eat off, had a replacement top and I had insufficient knowledge at that time to know. I knew several restorers, and without letting on, quizzed them as to how to make it look better. There was a general clam-up and a desire not to give their trade secrets away but I gathered that they

bought their supplies and concoctions from a London company by the name of Jenkins, so I secretly wrote for their list, which featured about 60 different things such as rotten stone, carbon black, gas black, oak powder and Stainax, so I had some of each and just experimented on Sunday mornings. Rotten stone is used for faking dust and when next I saw it I knew instantly that the item had been tampered with.

Back to how did I learn to recognise antiques in general? Well, taking the London sale catalogues and viewing their sales when I could helped, but most things I learned from taking strict observational rules from my own experience and listening to the voices of experience. To tell if the item was of its correct period, if it was, for instance, mahogany, I would look firstly at the metalwork fittings, asking myself if the screws were hand or machine made. This is always a good test. If there was any glass involved, I would look to see if there were any seeds and ripples visible, then I would know that it was old. Then I would look closely at the timber, because the early imported mahogany, i.e., about 1750 and the age of Chippendale, would be Cuban mahogany which has a very decorative swirling grain. Then as the supply of this and other mahoganies ran out, the grain became straighter and less interesting, such as from Honduras. I would guess that mahogany started being imported about the time of the slave trade. Along with turkeys and tobacco, occasional pieces of mahogany had been imported right back to the age of Drake and Raleigh, but this is extremely rare and shows in the price that it makes. I would also look at all tellers of time, these being the naturally accumulated dirt in the corners and watermarks, and if the use on its skin was genuine and not put on with chains and other false appliances.

I remember a refectory table with a wrong top that did not reach its reserve, so we stored it in the summer months in an old stable belonging to Mother at Newmarket. Unbeknown to us the building leaked, and it got rained on. When we brought it out for our first autumn sale without touching it, it realised about half as much more than the original reserve. In another sale we offered an oak refectory table that was so well faked that its age was difficult to tell. When the bidding in the saleroom reached £1,500 and some private people were going mad for it, I announced that it was not old but the bidding still continued. That was the last fake that we knowingly sold, as I felt that we were just selling our good name for the sake of money.

Marble seams have run out just the same way as the mahogany did. I am told that it is impossible now to buy statuary marble. This is as it indicates, but the difference between this and the white Carrara marble is that it can be fairly iridescent. This means that if you stand it in a window the outside sunlight can shine through it, giving a pleasing glow effect. Dates concerning when any of these things changed are important, so the cataloguer needs to have a keen sense of history.

About this time we received a small seventeenth-century oak gateleg table from Mrs Huddlestone of Sawston Hall, near Cambridge. Both the family and the Hall were ancient, and this table I guessed could have been in the Hall since birth, so to speak. It had a perfect crusted skin as outlined and I really rated it. Normally such tables would make about £400, but this one was special because of its originality, an originality that can only come from well-cared-for use.

When I opened the bidding there seemed a reluctance to bid, in spite of a crowd of dealers who stood together in a corner of the room. One dealer bid to about £350, then loudly said, "No more." I had suffered this 'no more' signal before and knew that it meant 'it is now your turn' to the other dealers but more important it was done to try and convince the auctioneer that their last bid was the value. It really raised my ire. Having pieces as pure as this in our saleroom meant a lot to me and I was not going to see its price murdered. There was a very quiet, insignificant, pasty-faced dealer named Brown, who came to our sale most times and who always stood with his dealer brethren, so when this lone bidder loudly shouted, "No more," I took the next bid off Brown, although he had not bid, then again and again until the real bidder stopped and I was in at £2,400. I then shouted the name Brown although I knew, and he knew, that he had not bid. Brown moaned that it was not him so I said, "Oh if there is a dispute I will put it up again," and asked for a bid of £2,000, at which point about half a dozen of those that were standing together shook their heads. I then started it myself at £2,000 and took longer than normal to be sure that I was giving everyone a chance before knocking it down and calling out quite loudly and plainly my own name. Brown and another dealer came up to the rostrum to tell me that they were not coming to my sales again. That night I put the table on the lorry of a regular carrier, together with an account for the price that I had knocked it down to myself at, and told the carrier to take it to a Mr X who was a very reputable London dealer. A cheque came by return with a note that said, "Thank you, Mr Lanham. It is a pleasure to do business with you."

One of the dealers who said that he was not going to come again phoned the next day and said, "You have not apologised to me yet." I apologised immediately because it is only a real friend who would do that. He then said, "If you were a dealer you would be in it, because you are a business man." "No," I said, "I do this for the love of it, I am so proud to have been able to present such untouched goods like this, and getting the optimum for my client brings me a lot more pleasure than money for the sake of it ever can."

On another occasion a dealer who I much respected came up to me before a sale and said, "I am very interested in a lot here. If I bid you will not run me will you?" I replied, "I would never run anyone who stands on their own two feet." I knew which lot it was, as I had semi-hidden it in the saleroom for him to 'discover'.

I knew, quite well, an English dealer who had a shop in Phoenix, Arizona. Although he sent things out there to sell, when there he would have a look around and buy what he could. He always gave me the pick of the things that he had bought to take for auction when he returned. A lot of these pieces had been bought for next to nothing because it seems that being of the period did not have the importance in the USA that it does here. This was borne out when we had a gold Jacobite ring for sale bearing hair of Donald MacDonald of Kinlochmoidart in Scotland. He had been aide-de-camp to Bonnie Prince Charlie when he first came over from France. After being captured by the dreadful Sassenachs, he was imprisoned in Carlisle, where, after the conflict, he was beheaded and his head displayed on the ramparts. I immediately thought that the American fast-food company McDonald's would be after this, so I approached them in one or two places but received no reply. I then found out that there was both a Scottish clans magazine, and a MacDonald magazine, in the United States, so I advertised in them accordingly. Both of these magazines were full of reproduction kilts and the standard kit to be worn, but I had no reply whatsoever for my interesting period ring from Americans, which disappointed given the American fast-food company which, despite its wealth, had exploited the name to their own advantage.

I am pleased to say the ring was bought by the Scottish Museum on the Isle of Skye for a few thousand. A distant member of the

MacDonald clan phoned about it and said that the only thing that the MacDonalds had left him was an island in the middle of a Scottish river. So he had gone up to see it and to do that he had got an old gilly to row him out to it. He got his map out, noticing that it had a big hill in the middle, he said to the gilly, "It's just six acres." "Oh no, no, no," said the gilly. "We measure land a lot different up here than you do in England. You see that big hill? Well, we measure up one side and down the other, then across ways up and down and you'll see when you work it out that it's at least seven acres and not six."

This tale reminds me of a Scotsman who delivered a piece of furniture one day and having a very thick accent I said, "What part of Scotland are you from?" "Arbroath," he replied. "I know it's where the fish come from," I said. "Oh no no no," he said, "the fish come from the sea."

I viewed Christie's sale in South Kensington one day and asked an old porter the way to the toilet, "If you go down the stairs and turn right," he said with a cheeky grin, "you'll see a sign upon a door that says Gentlemen, but take no notice of that sign you can still go in." That is the humour that I love and it used to abound all day in the sales of the prior culture.

It never ceases to amaze me how the majority of items that we got into our sales came out of complacency by the seller who did not know what they had got. Similarly, if it had been written in a will that all items were to be sold by Boardmans, we almost invariably never got them. The executors seemed to think that they knew better, so did it their way. I remember a local lady who had seen how well we had done for the trust where she worked, and so left instructions in her will that we were to sell her effects. She had a titled lady executor who phoned us to say would we take her things in our sale. "Of course we will," I said. "I know that she had some nice watercolours."

"Er I am afraid we have sent all those things to Perkins."

"Well how about her fine furniture?" I asked, to which she replied "Perkins have taken that as well."

"Then I think that Perkins should have the rest," I said. I had had enough of this infidelity. Similarly, if we had an executors' sale, I cannot think of an instance, where there was not friction somewhere. On one occasion someone who entered a piece in our sale told me that he was told that I would be difficult, but the man for the job. I can understand that.

In 1975, the two major London auctioneers introduced a dreadful thing called 'the buyer's premium'. What this meant was that if one deigned to give these auctioneers your patronage, then they would charge you 10% on top of the purchase price for the privilege of just being you, it seemed. Of course everyone protested at this imposition, and many were they who said they were going to boycott these firms altogether, but humans have human traits and their greed soon overcame them. I hated the very principle of it. All my career we had charged vendors only at the 15% if they were private vendors and 10% to the trade, no extras, and nothing if the item did not sell at an agreed reserve. It was the thin edge of the wedge and like Topsy it grew and grew. Having stuck it out as long as possible I was the last of the larger firms to introduce the premium about ten years after it had first come about, and when I did I found that it made no difference at all to the price which I again attributed to human frailty.

The buyer's premium has increased until together with the vendor's commission it has reached a situation in which the auctioneers remunerate themselves with almost half of the hammer price. If one is selling something with a fairly common trade price, such as gold for scrap, then there is not much sense in losing almost half its price in auctioneer's commission. However if the item that you are selling is very rare, then no one really knows what is in the head of both under bidder and the ultimate buyer, and in this case the realisation price should not be guessed at and the only place to sell it is through the auction rooms.

I remember selling some large eighteenth-century Dutch paintings of tea houses along the river, that had come out of a large local residence. They had been valued at very little. When we sold them for a lot of money, the vendor had questions from the tax authority. I worked it so that the vendor paid no more tax, and neither did anyone else who I acted for, who had similar problems. I found that these office wallahs, who sit within four walls all day, have distorted views of value. They probably get a figure from the statistics office that antiques have gone up by, say, 5% during the year. However, within that 5% some items will have increased by as much as 100% or 200% or more and others gone down in value by similar amounts. You cannot average out the price of antiques, for the factors that affect like for like are manifold. One must have research to argue like for like, and the little taxman cannot possibly have as much reference as you have. Remember that averaging takes much skill. Without this skill you will end up thinking that if you have one leg in the oven and the other in the freezer you will be okay on average. "The average man has less than two legs!" said Michael Caine. This should of course read "man on average".

We sold a painting of still life and birds once for a deceased estate. We estimated approximately what we thought that the collection could make for the solicitor, and then sent them the results. Most of the paintings realised within reason the price that we had estimated, but one painting by a well-known Dutch still life artist called Hondecoeter made over three times more than estimated. Why this solicitor should want to look a gift horse in the mouth I do not know, but we told him what we thought: that the painting was possibly a fragment, meaning that it was once part of a larger painting and had been trimmed for some purpose, or even cut in two. Given this, then it was worth very much less than its apparent 'book' value. This was borne out by the fact that it had sold to a private buyer bidding against another private buyer, whilst the trade abstained. You may think that we should have given this opinion in our catalogue, but if we had it would have killed the sale completely, and if you buy at auction one of the rules is 'caveat emptor – let the buyer beware'. However I do not feel that we had cheated or misinformed anyone.

On another occasion we sold an item for £3,000 that was now being shown in a major fair marked £12,000, and the press had phoned saying "Are you not embarrassed?" "No," I replied, "it is probably borrowed from the person who bought it from us, who would probably ask £5,000 for it from the stand holder. It has no doubt cost a lot of money for it to be presented at this major art fair and if it does not sell, then it could become blighted for it would be now well-known and back in the hands of the original purchaser, and the only recourse for him is probably to dump it in another auction and possibly take less than he gave for it."

There was a well-known company at this time who produced a Price Guide book once a year. They annoyed me, for whatever price we or any other auction rooms had sold an item at, they seemed to automatically think that we were the trade price and they would add a fixed percentage on for retail. The worst thing was that the public were guided by this guessing business and had no knowledge of the forces behind how the price had come about. They would have done well not to comment if they had known the reason why. What I am saying is that if they had any knowledge of the reason behind the price. i.e., Kipling's what, where, why etc., I would have thought that they would have realised that they were misleading their readers. As I was to learn from an old head: "Association with is not necessarily reason for."

Another fallacy is that to get the most advantageous price one should send the item back to the country of its origin. A lady who had lived in America but was now in UK sent to us a chest that she had bought in the States for £10,000. It was late seventeenth century, of standard form with a single rising lid, two drawers beneath, three-panel front and an all-over painted decoration typically known as Pennsylvania American. We advertised it in America and had several telephone lines booked. It was bought and underbid by Americans to go back there not

The 17th-century Pennsylvanian chest bought for £10,000 in USA sold by ourselves for £23,000 to go back to USA.

for £10,000 but £23,000. How was this price achieved? Simply by the psychology that the purchasers had, to their mind, 'discovered it'. Then they thought it should not be in our hick saleroom in England, so they thought they were 'saving' it. But you still need the skill of knowing where that buyer is most likely to come from.

In 1986 we had instructions to sell the contents of the boardroom of a local factory. This included several good paintings, one being by Alexis de Leeuw and another by the English-born New Zealand artist Charles Blomfield. The vendor said that he wanted us to handle the sale, but expected that we would either send it to New Zealand to be sold, if not London. I told him that we dearly wanted to handle the sale ourselves and that we would probably make more money in our saleroom in Clare than in New Zealand or London. I do not think that he totally believed us, but he had been badly treated by another auction concerning 'porter's perks' and his advisers had recommended us. We did our research and found that the highest price at that time for a work by Blom-field was £12,000 and that had been made by an auction house in New Zealand. Lorna Noble, our advertising agent, recommended that we advertise it in a certain New Zealand daily paper, which we did and had several phone lines booked to New Zealand as a result.

As expected I was pursued by estimate hunters but gave nothing away, saying only that it was a genuine reason for sale, was entered privately, and had not been seen in the trade. What more could anyone want I thought. Having said this, where estimates are not given I have always found it quite extraordinary how others think when left to their own devices. Also I have in the past checked to find that some estimates are wildly inaccurate. Whatever the estimate, this has no bearing on the price, so why give the public information that can only wildly guide them?

BUT DEAR, THE CATALOGUE DISTINCTLY SAYS 'SIGNED BENEATH A STONE, BOTTOM RIGHT HAND CORNER'

We sold the painting to a London gallery for £23,000, almost doubling the record. I felt that the reason this had made so much money could have been that when this notable London gallery had its colonial exhibition, it could not exhibit pictures by New Zealanders that were already known to the market – which they could assume was the case with the one they bought from us. Little did he know where we had advertised it!

CHAPTER 13

Oak and Its Skin

D uring 1985 I was asked to go and look at six former church pews. The vendor had taken an opinion from elsewhere and having been told that they were not 'of the period' he was not happy. He explained to me that they had come from Mickfield Church which is near to Debenham in Mid Suffolk. Period pews are about the oldest pieces of furniture that one can get, so I asked him how he had acquired them. He said that Mickfield Church was redundant and had a serious settlement crack running right the way down the tower to the ground, and that it had hardly been attended, so it had been de-consecrated and sold for very little on the understanding that the purchaser repaired the tower. Our vendor was the builder who had been asked by the purchaser to do a few repairs, and had been told that he could take the pews if he wanted them. The pews were six in total, and he had done nothing with them since acquiring them, and now asked us if we would sell them for him.

The first thing that I did was to ask the vendor if we could use the provenance and upon his approval I looked up the date of Mickfield Church as, in my opinion, these pews had been made to go in it. Having found that this date was late fourteenth century I duly advertised them for sale, only to find that I had opened up a can of worms. This church had been put up for sale because it was no longer being used and had stood vacant for a number of years, but now that the pews were being put up for sale many parishioners were coming out of the woodwork and demanding them back. They even reported us to the police who phoned, and on the view night aggressively told me that I was not to sell them. My reply was that I had the signed vendor's entry form confirming that they were his to sell and if they wanted me not to sell them then they must put it in writing, which they refused to do. The policeman that I spoke to did not like me standing up to him and told me that I would be getting a "visit from the police," whatever that meant.

We advertised them as being of fourteenth-century origin, but a man who called himself a 'leading authority on church furniture', on viewing had told everyone around him in the auction room that they were not of the period. It is a good job that I was not there at the time as he would have gone away with more than a flea in his ear. When he got home he duly wrote and made a claim on us for his wasted day out. I also found it amazing how some of our porters would rather believe him than me, and suggested that I should withdraw them. Not so, I replied and the following day I sold them for a total of £23,000. I politely wrote and told the 'leading authority on church furniture', saying that we all make mistakes from time to time. I sent no money of course and heard no more from him. If he had admitted his mistake I would have borne him no malice, but he did not have the decency to reply. Next I heard from the man who had originally owned the church, but he had not fulfilled the obligations that he had legally made to repair the tower, and I understand that the authorities foreclosed on him, taking the church back. They then sold it to a well-to-do third party to both live in and to hold church services. He came back to me asking how he could get some of the pews returned. I am pleased to say that I did acquire one for him from James Brett, a good customer

One of six 14th-century oak pews from Mickfield Church that sold for £26,000.

from Norwich. What a palaver! But the interesting thing to me was how could the other agent and the authoritarian church furniture man think that the pews were not old? The head of one of the mythological beasts on the end of one of the pews had been struck off, no doubt in the reign of Henry VIII during his dissolution of the monasteries, and this to my mind guaranteed their authenticity. But the mind boggles and such Doubting Thomases are no doubt still about!!

The first person who said that these pews were not of their period was our fiercest competitor – a representative from a London auctioneer, and at the time about the third biggest firm in the country. It had been reported to me that part of his spiel in getting goods away from us was to say the following: "Boardmans! Boardmans! Why send something to Clare when we can sell it for you in London." As I had heard this several times I thought that I would be ready with my reply for when I heard it again.

My reply was: "Price is about what people do, not where they live. The size of Clare and the size of London has nothing whatsoever to do with price, and if you or I went to the major salerooms in London to buy a lot, there is a feeling that if you get it then you have paid one bid more than the best buyer in the world and that is a turn off – bad psychology.

"But if that lot should come up for sale in a sleepy Suffolk Town Hall and you, a prospective purchaser, are made aware of it, there can be a feeling of discovery, and with it, a determination to secure it regardless. This creates a feeling of raiding the place, and if you should then see your biggest competitor across the room then it is usual to think, 'Oh blast. He's here but if he gets it I will make sure that he pays for it', – that psychology is usually worth double the London one."

Within myself I feel that this again is about understanding those bold grenadiers of Mr Kipling, this time as applied to exactly what influences market forces. The understanding of people, and what they are doing in this matter is vital, and that can only come from prolonged experience.

We sold a sixteenth-century carved oak figure that had been acquired by an old friend and retired dealer, Tom Smith, who had purchased it out of the cattle market pens at a sale in Bury St Edmunds in the mid-1960s. I believe that Tom had paid about £80 for it, and I was fairly sure that it had arrived where it did as a result of the death of a vendor who was an old client of ours. The naivety of this carving gave away the fact that it was not Flemish, as they are usually very finely carved, but English and it went on to another very good English dealer at £3,000. It is strange to accept that what could be considered to be the much poorer quality making more than the better quality one, but as Thomas Carlisle said, "The boulder in the path of the weak is a stepping stone for the strong!"

Also for Tom we sold four sixteenth to seventeenth-century carved oak cherub figures that once had formed the supports for a very fine oak dining table. These were Flemish and went to Holland for £10,300. He also asked us to sell for him a small mid-eighteeth-century ebonised bracket clock by William Allum of London. This was about four inches smaller in height than the usual, and Garrard, the appointed Royal Jewellers, came and paid a five-figure sum for it.

During the war, Tom had piloted gliders into Arnhem and when arriving on the other side of the deep and wide River Rhine was instructed to act as a bodyguard for a bigwig officer. He would sometimes play in goal in football matches for the Suffolk antique dealers against our arch enemies known as Norfolk antique dealers. I was usually asked to play as a guest. Believe you me this was a great honour, considering the circle of people that I was playing for. I particularly remember the away match because as we neared the Norfolk ground in our coach, one dealer's wife in her very Suffolk accent kept taking the mickey out of our absent hosts by saying, "Do you think we're all daft up here?" and "I hear that they've lost their village idiot and they are now all taking it in turns" and "It is terrible about things stolen from the Norwich City's football ground. The trophies room has been completely emptied and police are now looking for a green and yellow carpet." Poor old Norwich. It was great fun taking part in this revelry. Having lost a kneecap as a result of a car accident, I was told not to play football again, but this was worth breaking all the rules for.

Following the match and after a few ales we always had a sing-song. At the time I was playing my squeeze box in a country dance band and Tom would always request me to sing a song that I had made up about Alan Hunter the Ipswich centre back, who did not just put the ball into touch but hoofed it over the stand. Tom was particularly vocal on the chorus of "Anywhere will do."

I still have a Rowlandson print 'Mistake at Newmarket' hanging in my hall. It belonged to Tom and reminds me of those heady days of pure fun. We usually won of course!

The 16th-century, distinctly English carved oak saint that sold for £3,000.

In 1986, oak and early artefacts were still going great guns and on one occasion I advertised our sale as Boardman the 'oakioneers'. However, although I liked it I did not do it again, as I know how people think that as you sell one thing you cannot sell another. Stupid, is it not? But one must be aware of all these erroneous foibles. This is totally bogus thinking but it happens all the time. Such a thing happened one day when an old general dealer brought us a piece of period furniture and by chance I went outside to see him off. I saw, on the dashboard of his van, a pair of what looked like ormolu candlesticks. "What are you going to do with those?" I asked. "Well," he replied, "I thought that you did not sell brass so I was taking them to Mike up the road and I am going to put £40 reserve on them." A closer look revealed that they had a coat of arms and an inscription. I would like to do some research on these I said. "Can I sell them?"

"Of course" he said.

Now if you come across a coat of arms only a fool would sell anything without finding out whose coat of arms it is, because it could be from royalty or anyone. Research led to us finding out that the coat of arms was that of the Armourers and Braziers Company, one of the oldest livery companies in the city of London, and that the candlesticks had been presented to the company by the worshipful master upon his retirement from his position in 1757. I hunted through all my books to see if I could find anything quite like them. The nearest was in a book on brassware by Rachael Field and Belinda Gentle. I knew Rachael Field from when she sold us advertising space in a magazine, so I phoned her and also sent a photo to the keeper of metalware at the Victoria and Albert Museum in London, from whom I had received help in the past. The V&A wanted to buy them but did not think that they would be able to afford them, which made me prick up my ears. The date of 1757 on these sticks was important because their style was rococo, at a time when it was thought that English candlestick makers could not make candlesticks to rococo design like the French. Furthermore, they were open core cast, with a hole up the middle which was again a first for this period.

We duly advertised them to catch their most probable market. In the meantime I met Rachael Field in London and took her to the Armourers and Braziers Company to inspect their candlesticks. A gentleman in livery costume of black and grey answered the door and took us past umpteen suits of armour, to a table where their four pairs of candlesticks had been put for us to inspect. An examination revealed that one pair were a slightly different size from the other three pairs, so I assumed that our pair must

The pair of 18th-century brass candlesticks ex the Armourers and Braziers Company that realised £11,000 to go to America.

have gone missing at some time and the oversized pair were a recast. It is possible that they had been stolen a long time ago, but if they were, no one knew any difference so we carried on with our sale. However I later discovered that they had been bought from a modest house in a local village wrapped in an old rag and hidden in a cupboard under the stairs.

I remember the day well because the bidding was taken up by Belinda Gentle against Richard Jorgensen of Maine, USA. Gentle stopped at around £3,000 and Jorgensen carried on until he bought them at £11,000, bidding against a phone line. After the sale the phone bidder called to ask who had bought them and when we said Richard Jorgensen she said, "Oh please don't tell him, we were only bidding to sell them to him." Jorgensen later revealed that he would have gone to £15,000, so how do you work out the value from that? Our research led us to be able to answer fully all six of the questions asked by Kipling's six honest serving men, and that was rare.

In 1989 we were to have another fine pair of candlesticks make a lot of money. We described them as being of mixed metal and they had been made by Tiffany and Co. of New York, circa 1878. They had a central round knop of one metal bleeding through another so that it makes regular patterns which I believe from memory is known as macrame work. Around this time the most sought-after designer, Christopher Dresser, had gone to Japan to bring back items for Tiffany's and we tried to associate them with his influence. Dresser was a man ahead of his time and his influence goes on. He laid down historic principles as to what fine art should represent. From an 1862 report the two that come to mind are:

"Utility must precede beauty" and "Many brutes can copy but only a few can create."

The candlesticks were sold to an international silver dealer for £24,000 and we believe that, weight for weight, was another international record.

One day a vendor, from the West Country, who we knew well, phoned and said that he had a Wrotham tyg that he was going to send to us to go in our next sale. Apparently he was selling it for someone else and had taken an opinion from one of the major London auctioneers who had said that it should make around £1,500. A Wrotham tyg is simply a jug in early English pottery made in the south of England village of Wrotham. It is something like slipware and what

The pair of late-19th-century silver candlesticks by Tiffany of New York that sold for £24,000.

makes it collectable is that it usually has an inscription and often a date (a where, how, and when!). Some are early eighteenth century, but this one was late seventeenth century, which is an advantage. But it had been damaged and repaired, which is a serious disadvantage. The sale was duly advertised, but about a couple of days before the sale a lady from the West Country phoned to say that the lot was hers and she wanted a reserve of £8,000. I protested but she became quite abusive as though we were trying to cheat her. I had read that a Wrotham tyg of this age had made that price at auction, but that price was for one that was apparently perfect, ours was not. I told our contact that this had happened and all he said was "Let me make some enquiries." I knew that our buyer's premium would be 10% so I thought that I would forgo that and take £7,200 which would have made the same amount to her.

We struggled in the selling but finally got to this price so I let it go, feeling quite relieved. A solicitor, acting for the lady vendor, now came on the phone demanding that we pay his client the full £8,000 and would not let me explain at all. On speaking to the gentleman who had sent the item to us he then explained that the person who appeared to own the lot was a lady who would live in with elderly people and look after them in their later years. Our gentleman had been to see the family who she had last worked for, to find that she had no right to the tyg at all, and had in fact been given something else but definitely not this. The next day a letter arrived from another solicitor saying that his deceased client was the rightful owner of this tyg and would we kindly account to him, which we duly did. The alleged lady helper got nothing and was lucky not to find herself on the wrong side of 'Newgate knocker'! Of course, no apology was forthcoming from her solicitor.

I remember this sale quite well as this item along with other smalls had been on display in the basement and had to be brought up individually as was the tyg. I do not think that anyone in the room would think that this old, damaged item could have made as much as it did and after it had been sold, and as the porter turned the corner to take it back to the basement there came an extremely loud sound of breaking pottery, which caused much mirth in the saleroom as the company all thought that the porter had dropped it. Not so. The porters had left an old chamber pot on the concrete steps for one of them to smash by kicking it. The expensive tyg had not been affected and this was just another porter's joke.

The Dutch oak market suddenly crashed and by the end of the 1970s was virtually finished. Why this should be I do not really know, but it was something like the rush for tulips in Holland of the seventeenth century, which likewise hit the dust after seeing a phenomenal drop in value. I think if it had been here in the UK it would not have been so drastic, but it seemed a specialised and delicate market for Dutch things in Holland. The UK would have been a more worldly market and more supportive I feel. I understand that one dealer had about 50 of these big cupboards in stock, so he halved the price, and sent as many as he could get into auction sales, because "there are always people about who will not know that the trade has fallen." However, Dutch dealers stopped coming and when the market had settled, would you believe it, we had a phone call from a Mrs Mommersteeg in Holland, saying could they send some pieces of English oak back for us to sell. Her husband had died, and she had three barns full. It was good business for us.

Also about this time we suddenly had a dealer from Spain come into the saleroom. I think that during the period of Franco's rule few antiques had been allowed into, or out of, Spain, but they had now joined the Common Market and apparently received big money for the improvement of roads and the like, and this in turn had caused a new class of entrepreneurial rich.

We had some pieces sent to us from a dealer in Canada and one day he sent a large pair of seventeenth-century Venetian carved and gilt door frames. These we sold to a new private Spanish buyer for £39,600. This Spanish buyer and his dealer friend now bought furniture across the board, such as period tables and chairs in mahogany, walnut and oak, also chests on stands, a mahogany library table for £6,800, paintings, a small walnut bureau at £7,000, and two English

One of a pair of 17th-century Italian door portals which were sent to us by a Canadian dealer and we sold to a private Spanish buyer for £40,000.

189

seventeenth-century wainscot armchairs for £3,900. I can remember
a dealer from Madrid competing with another from Barcelona in
the same way as we had Belgians bidding against Germans during
the oak boom. This Spanish dealer was now our best buyer and was
bidding against all others, so I gave him a 1% deduction from his
buyer's premium. This was the only time that I had done this, but he
did not show appreciation and it was money direct from our pocket.

In 1979 Margaret Thatcher and the Conservative Party came to
power and in due course she sold off what the former prime minister,
Harold Macmillan, called 'the family silver'. This gave a right for
people, in occupation, to buy council houses at modest prices, likewise shares in state-owned utilities such as gas, electricity and water,
which some people deemed belonged to all of us. These appeared to
be for modest prices. The money went into the government coffers
and came back to us to spend by way of lower taxes and other bene-
fits. It created an extraordinary demand for British things by British
people. It was largely 'in house' trading. The price of those things
that we demanded rose to an unprecedented level, and there came
a stronger consciousness of our homes and the cultural things that
we wanted to put in them. Prices of all items that were wanted by
the British rose like never before, and items came back to us from
Canada, Australia and New Zealand and USA by the container load.
The pound rose in the exchange rate to $2.40. But was this really a
false demand, for the government had simply taken money out of
the capital account to put it in the flagging profit and loss account, I
thought. Ours however was not to wonder why, but make the most of
it. Whereas in the 1970s, British people had stood aghast in the saleroom at the increase in prices from European buyers, they now had
cash in their pockets to jingle and this caused a hike in the things that
they wanted for their houses and gardens. A strange old world, but it
all reminds you that everything is firstly about people and in our case
what people are doing according to the politics of the day. On 10th

October 1992 I wrote a half-page personal view for the *Antiques Trade Gazette* that said just that.

James was a young porter who was anxious for a full-time job with us. He had been to help once or twice at sales and got on well, but more importantly, he knew that I was a chartered surveyor and he needed to be with a chartered surveyor to do some professional work to qualify for taking his exam. My wife Hazel had come into the firm as my secretary now that our twin children, George and Kate, were at school, and apart from Pip Harding, who did most jobs and was our bidding clerk on sale days, we had no other full-time help. The job of

Twins George and Kate helping Daddy to catalogue.

bidding clerk was introduced by Alan Fitchett. What this meant was that any person who wished to leave an absentee bid would now no longer leave it with the auctioneer to execute, but with an independent person who would faithfully bid on their behalf. If she had a lot of bids then she would need to get a second person to bid as well to ensure that the lot made the same price as if the bidder was in the saleroom.

At this time I had a kneecap removed following a car accident and was told not to play competitive sport again. I was highly frustrated so taught myself to take a football match down in shorthand and then took a part-time job with Wimbledon Football Club as their Team Performance Analyst. They were then under the management of Dave Bassett and were on the rise up the leagues. I loved it and like the antique sales I was always breaking new ground with discoveries that I believed no one else had done before. As in the antiques, I embraced the new technology and had what I believed to be the most advanced computerised programme. I could now analyse every touch of the ball and could print out the patterns of chance over a single match performance, or even a whole season, which was a revelation in itself.

I now had to watch two calendars very carefully and I got in a muddle once. I had written to George Graham, the manager of Arsenal, and got the job to fully analyse a sample of ten games for him. I was also preparing a sale at the time, so looked quickly at the date of the next Saturday game and on reading that it was at West Ham, put it out of my mind until I arrived at the West Ham ground – fortunately my usual one hour early on Saturday at 2pm. There was no one there. I looked all around and then discovered my mistake. The West Ham fixture was a League game, and this was a Cup game, which took precedence, and Arsenal were fortunately at home and I had not had the time to check. I got in my car and drove at speed, map book in hand, north through East London, which is a difficult route. Then I could find nowhere to park, but I kept driving, guessing the right direction, then parking on the side of the road. I fully expected to get a parking ticket. I then ran until my legs got the splints, with my feet just flapping. I saw the uniformed doorman, quickly showed him my director's box ticket and then ran into the marble halls of this beautiful art deco building, past the bronze bust of the great Herbert Chapman, then turned to go up the stairs. The team were now out and lining up, but I could see that someone was in my seat, so I headed in his direction regardless. When I arrived, a gentleman from a seat behind now said "Would you mind sitting over there, I am a director here?!" I clambered over a seat to sit next to a gentleman with a large nose wearing an expensive-looking camel coat but the worst, yes the worst, was yet to come. My new compatriot was smoking the largest possible cigar and as this smoke was collecting in my deflated lungs they kicked off. I recovered to do the job thinking as usual of a proverb, of course this being "That which hurts teaches."

We had got down to three sales the year before James arrived, which was not enough to earn our oats, so Hazel said to me why don't you give James a chance? I agreed his pay and told James that he would sit at a desk in my office and hear all that I said to every client, but he would have to be prepared to drive our small pantech-nicon van, and he agreed. We now had to get back to having five sales a year. That is three in the spring and two in the autumn. I knew of a biggish dealer in the north, who Alan Fitchett had introduced to our firm. He was always keen to put lots into our sales so I made contact and James drove the van up north whilst I, having had a late night, had a sleep in the back.

We were very careful about what we took from our dealer friend, but I wanted a star lot for the front of the catalogue. So at risk of people knowing where they had come from, we took the four matching eighteenth-century North Italian black walnut chairs which we advertised in the Continental magazine, *Weltkunst,* and had good enquiries from Southern Germany. I remember the sale well because a certain Italian dealer, whom I knew from causing a ruckus in the saleroom many years before, walked along the front about six lots before the chairs were to be sold, and when I called for order said to me, "You think people are chickens." I remembered him from old when he would intimidate anyone who dared to bid against him. Then he would stand up and shout across the room to his colleague, "We go now, Ferdi, it is too expensive here," but he would still bid and if you were going up in hundreds he would shout "ten".

He had got my goat now as all these things came flooding back. He then walked along and sat in an elm chair dug out of a tree trunk, a good piece of country furniture that we had just sold for £8,000, but he would not rate it at all. I told him not to break our furniture as he arbitrarily tried to rock it. He took no notice, so I shouted again. This time he said "Who? You meena me?" "Yes," I said, "don't break our furniture" and at this he slowly got up and walked out.

One of a set of four 18th-century North Italian Block Walnut chairs sold for £32,000 to a German dealer.

We sold the chairs to a dealer from Southern Germany for £32,000. He was bidding against a phone bidder. It may seem to those who did not know our history that I was overaggressive to this poor little man. Looks however can be wildly deceptive. One needs to know the history before making judgement. Of course you do not want upsets in the saleroom, but the auctioneer must at all times retain control. I was still apprehensive about this Italian and his friends but when I told the story to an old dealer who knew him he said, "Don't worry about it. He will respect you for standing up to him." Phew!

James got on well and the next big job we got was the clearing of Sir Frederick Ashton's House, Chandos Lodge, that lay behind the distinctively Suffolk red-brick wiggly wall in Eye near Diss. Sir Frederick was the well-known ballet choreographer. This again was a recommendation but there was so much that was interesting, but not of the highest value. Two lots of London auctioneers had already had their pickings, but James and I wanted to do it as it was a prestigious job. We just could not handle it all so sent a lot of smaller pottery items to Michael Dyson, another auctioneer who we worked with, and who had more general sales also in Clare. We often sent lesser lots on to Mike who was a friend, the only trouble being that the next time that local vendors had something for sale they sent them to Mike and many of these lots we would dearly like to have handled. I had stickers printed showing the provenance on each of Ashton's lots, for those that just wanted a token of remembrance. We made two mistakes in the cataloguing, but this was because we followed the

"YES, THANK YOU ERIC. BUT JUST HOLDING THEM UP WILL SUFFICE"

two separate leading auctioneers from London who had gone before us. We erroneously thought that they would have taken these lots had they been right, which they apparently were. A lesson to be learned I feel. These under-catalogued pieces did however make very good money and again I believe that in the pieces not being catalogued to the full could well have been a 'turn on' for the bargain hunter. There were some really good, unexpected prices, and the vendors, who were not expecting much, having had the two other auctioneers round, were very, very delighted. I am not at liberty to reveal the extent of the lady vendor's appreciation on the telephone when I told her the total that the sale had realised, but shortly after this, three complementary tickets arrived for a prestigious Sadler's Wells ballet performance.

In the house we had found about a dozen letters from the Queen Mother to Freddy, some with her quite exquisite pen and ink drawings in, but the vendor would not let us sell those. I remember queues and queues of people waiting to pay at the auction sale. We had sold things before for Shirley, Lady Beecham, the wife of the late Sir Lawrence, but those items had not been appreciated like these. The 'one lot' buyers had obviously only bought a keepsake each, but it seemed as though they made contacts with likeminded people who they would keep in touch with after the sale. The trail of buyers led from the downstairs accounts department, around the room then up the stairs into the saleroom and halfway round it, and chatter – you should have heard them. I was so overawed with the occasion that I did not say a word about order, the ambience was that special.

Looking back at the sale, what pleases me most is that we sold Sir Frederick Ashton's ballet shoes to the Bata shoe museum in Canada and Dame Margot Fonteyn's to Japan. In the old part-time estate agency days things seemed to be just advertised in the local rag and expected to sell themselves after that. This was well before the internet and things could well have changed hands six or eight times before they reached the man at the end of the line – the world's most likely buyer, but I felt that we had done this in one and it was proof that my ambition was almost certainly fulfilled. Dame Margot Fonteyn's ballet shoes had inscribed upon them 'Thank you Freddie for a wonderful Ondine'. In sending them both to the other side of the world showed that now we really were international. I remember phoning Freeds, the ballet shoe makers, about Dame Margot's shoes. The person on the other end of the line knew straight away and instantly said, 'Size 4 pink satin' and I thought that was how they labelled her!

Sir Frederick had an Aubusson carpet which was threadbare. He was a friend of the Queen Mother and an uninvited newspaper photographer had snapped the state of this carpet through a window. We hung it up in the saleroom so that its full state could honestly be shown. Threadbare or not, it still made £1,500 to the carpet trade. I can only think that it was still saveable and would most probably have ended up at the Aubusson carpet organisation for a complete overhaul – how interesting are the lengths that anyone will go to if the object is highly sought-after. This sale was damned hard work, but the heartfelt appreciation showed by the lady vendor when I told her their quite unexpected total made my heart glow with pride. This however was not the highest price that we made in this expansive era and that was soon to follow.

Other good lots that we received at this time came from the Newmarket racehorse trainer Jeremy Hindley. It was again a recommendation. The lot that I remember most is the eight-day walnut long-case clock by Joseph Knibb. Knibb was clockmaker to King Charles II, so it was early in the history of clock making and Knibb was reckoned to be second only to the great Thomas Tompion. I found it amazing how many people came to inspect it, just to find out what he had done differently to other clockmakers. In other words to get into the maker's mind. Most of them were not interested in buying it but just wanted to know the difference, and trying to think as Knibb would have thought at that time. Jeremy Hindley told us that it had been valued for insurance at

The 17th-century walnut longcase clock by Joseph Knibb, clockmaker for Charles II, that sold for £73,000.

£25,000 by a major London firm of valuers but had complacency crept in again? This valuation must have been out of date for it realised £73,000 at our Clare sale.

I remember the occasion quite well because when the purchaser had first phoned to book a phone line, it being our last line left, I had asked him to give us a minimal indication of his bid, which he did, showing that he was a serious buyer. I did this because at a previous sale a London clock dealer had booked a line just to see how much the lot realised, I believed that he had no intention of bidding at all. If he had known the difficulties that we had to overcome to make phone lines available to all prospective bidders, I like to think that he would not have abused this service. We had five lines of our own, then two that we hired for the day from private people who lived on either side of the Town Hall. After that it was mobile phones from whoever we could get, even trustworthy porters. Mark, from Haverhill, who gave up a day from his office because he enjoyed helping us out, would take two lines of phone bidders which is a very difficult thing to do, particularly if they are both bidding at the end. We made Barry Richards, a fireman from Bury St Edmunds, our foreman porter. He had worked for us part-time a number of years, so he knew the frailties and pitfalls. He would be night watchman on the night before the sale and spent a lot of the night organising and laying phone lines for the away bidders which was just as well as we had our best lot yet about to appear.

CHAPTER 14

World Record Chairs

Y et another recommendation saw me go and view a set of 12 eighteenth-century Chippendale mahogany dining chairs at Tissington Hall, Ashbourne, Derbyshire, belonging to Sir John Fitzherbert. These were in the Gothic manner with cluster column front legs united by an 'H' stretcher, with three Gothic arches to the back, six Gothic arches supporting the arms on each side and stuff-over upholstered seats. These chairs were very rare and I knew of them as they were illustrated in an important book by Percy MacQuoid entitled *A History of English Furniture: The Age Of Mahogany*. The recommendation had come from the valuer for the Tissington Hall estate, and I agreed with him a reserve of £50,000. This was a lot of money, and the only yardstick that we had as a reserve was that a set of period Chippendale chairs, but not Gothic, had sold recently in the London auction rooms. It had come to our attention that whilst oak and seventeenth century and earlier furniture had been favoured by the European market, furniture from the eighteenth century and later was favoured by the Americans, which one can understand, as it is of the period of their history. Furthermore, the best mahogany originated in Cuba, and the Caribbean area nearby, then as it ran out it had been Honduras.

I wished that I had thought that one out when I was interviewed by Tony Scace of Anglia TV during the oak boom. I had been sitting on my own in a room in Norwich and told that it was going out live, which as you can imagine had not helped my nerves. It was immediately after a sale, and I was already exhausted, and was then rushed into the studio to be immediately asked "Why oak?" and the only thing that I could do was waffle as I was completely unprepared and had not thought it out!

I managed to find out the name of the buyer of the previous set of eighteenth-century Chippendale chairs that had appeared in the London rooms and we made sure that he received a catalogue. We

Two of the set of 12 Chippendale Gothic chairs that sold for £85,000 to an American buyer.

advertised our chairs with a photo in the *New York Times* and lo and behold, a dealer from King's Road, London came up to view them to advise a particular New York client. He in fact bid and bought them over the telephone for the princely sum of £85,000. This too was a record price, and I was glad to get away from the oak stigma that had been hung upon us, and now wanted to sell good lots of all kinds of furniture across the board.

It is a sad part of this business that one hears about interesting people like Sir Frederick Ashton after they are dead. Another such person was Harry Redvers Taylor. I received solicitors' instructions to go and inspect his bungalow, to find that it had been designed by himself all on one level floor for easy access in wheelchairs. Apparently he had arranged for his wife to go to a rest home whilst he had booked himself into hospital to have a hip joint replaced, but sadly he had never come round from the operation. There was room for only a little furniture in the house, apart from a fine eighteenth-century French walnut provincial encoignure cartonnier – a bow-fronted corner cabinet with clock surmount. There was a collection of modern first-edition books which we made a separate sale of. Included was a number of letters from Robert Graves, which proved that he was, or had been, in love with Mrs Redvers Taylor. There were rugby caps showing that Redvers Taylor had played for his country; a jacket belonging to Gertrude Stein, and a photograph of her in it playing the piano; and a collection of sculpture that he had made and exhibited at the Lefevre Gallery and elsewhere, made from recycled agricultural machinery parts.

The beneficiaries were the husband and wife who had written 'Alfie'. There were files on how he had made new discoveries of many different insects when stationed on an island as part of his army duties, and we had many phone calls from people just wanting to talk about him. One woman said, "He was the ugliest man in the British Army but the most loved." I indeed would love to have met him.

Concerning the people that you 'meet' when they are no longer with us, I love to go into a home where the contents have been undisturbed for two or more generations, as I find the things that the family have naturally clustered around themselves in the flotsam and jetsam of life tell an interesting tale of people, their desires and habits, that are relevant to the changing times that they are in. What I mean is that it could be argued that to see pieces outside of the context that they were initially bought to go into at the time, is like viewing a fish out of water. It is difficult to describe but it could also be said that it is like when Buffalo Bill brought the Red Indian Geronimo to exhibit in London he was not within his natural surroundings and was out of his context.

We had managed to get away from the oak-only stigma, and back to the sort of goods that went well in English homes. For a local gentleman, whose father had been the mayor of Bedford, and who had an extensive collection, we had in almost every sale various weights and measures. There was a bronze quart measure dated 'primo mai 1707' which was the date of the Act of Union between England and Scotland, and was highly sought-after at £5,300. It was rare because it was believed to have been cast in Stirling in Scotland. We also sold a number of late-sixteenth and seventeenth-century bronze wool weights from the same source and these made varying prices of between one and two thousand each. They were generally shield-shaped and were pierced with a hole at the top, so that they could be hung from either side of

A bronze quart measure believed to have been cast in Stirling, Scotland, sold for £5,300.

a saddle. I always imagined the king's men riding at speed into a marketplace where wool was being sold, shouting "Have at thee" as they dismounted from their horses, with these standard weights in hand when they had come to check that all the merchants' weights were correct.

We had an oil painting come in that we were sure was by the much sought-after horse artist John Frederick Herring, although it was not signed. It was ideal in its subject in that it was in a heathland setting, the horse was being held by the trainer and the jockey, having dismounted, was on his way to the weighing room with the saddle. It did, however, have a serious tear to the canvas across the horse's head. We had a phone call about it from the most likely purchaser, a London gallery which said that they could not get down to view it. I said that if that was the case then I would send it up to them. I got Lenny, a driver for our removal company, to take it in the back of my estate car to this dealer's gallery and to wait outside for it, which he did. The owners of this gallery were the underbidders. The purchaser was a private gentleman from the south of England, who paid just under £30,000 for it. He said that he would rather buy it in its unrestored state and have it restored himself so that he knew for certain all that had happened to it. I am not saying that this was the case here, but it is always best to sell both furniture and pictures unrestored. There is always the case that the buyer believes that he knows who and how to save it, whereas if it has already been restored the ego trip for them has gone, so has the story and, in spite of whoever does it, it will not have been restored to their liking.

About the same time we had the remaining contents of Denston Hall, near Newmarket, for sale. This was a very large house that had a hall on each of its four sides. On each of these landings there was an eighteenth-century German mahogany shrank (cupboard) but the market for these had been missed and every cupboard had stood there so long that as soon as we touched them they seemed to shed mouldings like confetti, as the fish glue that held them had disintegrated. The purchasers did not wish to keep the marble fireplace which had come from Palace House, Newmarket, the home of Charles II, and this we sold for a five-figure sum.

When the vendor said that he had offered the contents of the library to the purchasers of the house for what seemed to me to be a modest sum, I begged him not to let them go, as there could be anything in there, and told him that I would get in a book cataloguer and make a special book sale featuring these items alone. Denston Hall was the home of Mrs Harvey Leader. Harvey Leader was a Newmarket racehorse trainer, but the family had descended on the female line, and this included not only Clive of India but also Colonel Jefferson of Dullingham House, who had sailed from Woodbridge, Suffolk, to colonise the island of St Kitts – everyone being Suffolk born. Dunn-Gardner was the name of the family that had lived in Denston Hall before Harvey Leader, and they had been well-known collectors.

We arranged to have a specialist book expert catalogue the sale and amongst loads of interesting estate papers concerning manorial rights of hay-bote and plough-bote, and things such as an eighteenth-century bill for hanging a man etc., she found a small book containing 12 etchings featuring the story of Noah and the Ark by Johannes Wierix, who was a pupil of Albrecht Dürer, which we were quite excited about. These were advertised as usual, and we had a phone call from an American asking if he could view them on the Sunday before the sale. Normally this was not possible, as I really needed my rest, but we made special arrangements for him to come to my home with his family to view them. Apparently they had all been to a wedding in London the day before. I am glad that I put myself out because he bought them over the telephone for the sum of £98,000, which caused a shockwave and a round of applause in the saleroom. The Suffolk County Council had been interested in some papers by Lord Cornwallis who had local interests and who was deemed to have

Part of the set of 12 engravings by Johannes Wierix sold for £98,000 to an American buyer.

lost us the Americas, but unfortunately the lots realised more than they were prepared to pay. As a supporter of my county I would have helped them if I could by not charging a buyer's premium.

Whilst in the north of England I called on an old picture dealer. He had not asked to put anything in the sale but I just called to say hello as I passed his shop. After looking round he took me down in his cellar to show me a suit of armour that he had taken in part exchange for a picture. He was selling it quite cheaply, so as it looked the part I said that I would take it and have a go with it in a sale. It had an interesting looking pointed visor, and although he would have taken only £4,000, and there are many fakes about, I thought that it had a chance. It realised £10,000 and it was reported to me that shortly after the sale it was displayed in the window of Holland and Holland the famous London armourers. By chance I happened to bump into the man who came to bid for it. He lived quite locally and in chatting he revealed that he could not believe the suit of armour when he first saw it and reckoned that only himself and one other person were capable of recognising what it was. It was fifteenth to sixteenth-century Italian suit of armour – the Renaissance period – and a tiny number on the shoulder had told him that it was from a Tuscan town, where it would be brought out each year for the carnival. As with the Armourers and Braziers Company rococo brass candlesticks, I asked myself how did it get away from Tuscany into the possession of a collector, who not knowing what it was, swopped it with a fine art dealer, who knew absolutely nothing about it, who then gave it to us who knew a little more, and then to the buyer who knew exactly what it was? Could it have been misplaced in the war years? Complacency rules I tell you! You only have to look at *Antiques Roadshow* on the BBC on a Sunday night, where I would guess about a third of the pieces have been bought at a car boot sale for peanuts and another third at least I would guess the owners are equally unaware as to the value of what they have.

About this time the English trade had become exceedingly strong again and for one trade client we sold every lot, which produced him over £100,000 worth of mahogany, all in one sale. Rightly or wrongly, it seemed like Mrs Thatcher's doing, in 'Selling the family silver'! Every lot had sold and a very high proportion had gone to private English buyers direct. I did not really approve of what Mrs Thatcher was doing as it seemed to me that she was taking money out of the nation's capital account to be put into an ailing profit and loss account. Nevertheless it paid good dividends for us.

The American trade was also coming back strongly and this sale included a small George I walnut chest of four long drawers at £21,000. These remained in England, but a pair of glass ships' decanters with the name of the ship inscribed, sailed to America at £2,900. A Gainsborough chair similarly went into the American trade at £33,000, which must have been a record. It had come from the house of a very old dealer of the old school, who prided himself that he had bought out of all the best houses in Norfolk and also that he regularly entertained Queen Mary to tea. A Gainsborough chair has elbow arm supports, a padded back and seat. An average one would normally make about a £1,000–1,500, but this one was special because around the seat, the mahogany show frame was shaped and finely carved, as were the four cabriole legs. This a lay person would probably think was just a bit better, but look at the difference in price. The important principle here is that it is very difficult to appreciate the enormous difference in price between the fairly good piece and the very good piece. In this case you could say that it was almost 20 times the monetary price.

There was also a pair of Gainsborough chairs we sold one time to an East Anglian dealer, who phoned up about a week after the sale saying, "You know those chairs that you sold me as a pair, well, they do not match." I immediately said, "You are a bit late, but I will give you your money back. Please bring them back straightaway and I will then have the cheque ready," to which he replied, "I don't have them now but I will get them," which made me start getting suspicious. So I said, "If you don't have them, where are they?" With this

The George II mahogany Gainsborough chair that sold for an amazing £33,000.

and a further enquiry from a third party I found that he had let a runner take them around the country trying to sell them. After I heard this I refused to take them back, for the world and its cousin would now know all about them and this dealer had blighted them.

We also sold a set of 12 Regency mahogany dining chairs to a dealer who had the seats re-covered, and apparently when the upholsterer took the old covers off he found that there was original wheat straw stuffing, so it still had the ears of grain. He planted some, and surprisingly, despite being 200 years old, started to shoot. I gather that the ultimate purchaser was a private gentleman who manages the Princes Trust and that he in turn told the then Prince of Wales who, apparently, now has some of this wheat growing at his Highgrove Estate. Do you think that we deserve the royal appointment?

I was asked to value a pair of satinwood card/tea tables. They were in store in an East Anglian furniture depository, and I recall that we had some previous lots from this vendor that were always of top quality. The vendors were disappointed by the valuation from a local firm of £3,000 I believe, so they had come back to ourselves. The tables were of extremely fine quality and both of them had an unusual swing leg that was hinged by a metal rod running down the centre of another leg. This is something that I believe could not happen with mahogany, but satinwood of this Regency period is very hard and durable. Their quality reminded me of the royal cabinetmakers, Holland and Sons, that made a lot of furniture for Buckingham Palace. The vendor wanted absolutely no publicity for her sister, so I am not at liberty to tell you all, but they were bought by the well-known London dealer, 'Dick' Turpin, for £27,000 and when I spoke to him at a wake, following the funeral of a much-respected friend and dealer Ralph Cox, he told me that those were exactly his thoughts.

We had a call from the owners of a large residence near Braintree called Glazenwood which sounded as if it could result in a private sale at the residence. To try and impress on such a prestigious occasion, I

A pair of Regency satinwood tables believed to have been made by Holland and Sons, that realised £27,000.

took with me both my secretary and head porter Barry. I remember waffling on about my competitors who had already viewed, when the vendor stopped me and said, "But you do not know that." He was right and it made me realise that I was trying to pull the wool over his eyes. Our competitors had agreed to sell all general items for free in a local saleroom and take the rest to their London salerooms – a fat lot of good they are doing the area I thought. I am pleased to say that we won the day and duly held a general sale on a Saturday at the house which went well, and saved the paintings and furniture for our collective sale at Clare. The highlight of their furniture was an eighteenth-century walnut hall table with four cabriole legs under a marble top. The interesting thing was the Italian marble top, which was from a seam that had long since run out called breccia viola,

An 18th-century walnut table with rare breccia viola marble top. £20,000.

which was a purple colour. It was this that caused it to go to a London dealer at the unexpected sum of £20,000.

In this sale we also sold an early eighteenth-century marquetry barometer for £3,400, a nineteenth-century ship's barometer with gimbal in a case, which included many notes as to which ship it had been on – this made £1,650. We also sold a Georgian mahogany bow front barometer for £1,000. A private English buyer had paid the extraordinarily good price of £24,000 for an early eighteenth-century laburnum oyster wood cabinet of drawers mounted upon a stand of a shallow drawer over five twist legs. Yes, English money was about again.

Talking of people taking the best out of the area, whilst viewing London sales I had seen other auctioneers local to us in Suffolk taking good lots to be sold up there in the smoke, as we say down here, which is something that we would not do. With anything and everything that we found locally, I always made sure that these lots were sold in Suffolk by ourselves, so that anyone coming to our auctions would know that the best had not been creamed off. I think that one owes that to your buyers – and of course my belief is that they would probably get a better price with us in any case. We had not had any good pictures entered for some time, but out of the blue came a completely unexpected call.

CHAPTER 15

Harley of Harley Street

C olonel Harley who lived in North Essex, phoned one day saying that he had a collection of paintings, and asked if would we go to see them, which we duly did. On arrival he handed us a handwritten scroll of several pages which informed us that the collection had been put together by one of his relatives who had been in a high-ranking position with Charles I. The great typewritten notes that he handed round, made us think these pictures had probably been offered before and the market for them had been a bit overcooked and blighted.

We took the paintings in and arranged a special sale around them at the Corn Exchange, Bury St Edmunds. There were about 40 or 50 good paintings in total and we sold most of them quite well. However, we had no bid for what was potentially the most important painting – a very large life-size portrait of Charles I by Sir Anthony Van Dyck and the reserve was £10,000. We had taken an opinion on it and had been advised not to fully attribute it, as there was more than one copy of this picture in existence. I think that the Harleys were fairly pleased overall, in spite of the lack of interest in the Van Dyck.

About three years later the vendor asked if we would have another go at selling this picture with a reserve of £5,000 and again we had no interest. Another three years passed and again the picture was entered, this time with a reserve of £2,500 with discretion. Again it failed to sell, and I believe that it was because by this time it had become absolutely blighted. We had a dealer who would have a go at most things and would go round with me after a sale looking at most unsold lots, for which he would often buy or make an offer. The day after the sale he phoned to offer £1,000 for the attributed Van Dyck which the Harleys accepted. He displayed it at a profit in his East Suffolk shop when, lo and behold, a buyer took it away and after much research was able to declare it to be right and by the hand of Van Dyck!

There are several lessons here I feel. One is that these things all have a shelf-life in the cut and thrust of when and how they come onto the market. Two, that all the razzmatazz was no good for it. It would have been better if it was 'discovered'. The story about Harley of Harley Street is typical of what could be 'made up', and therefore sounded too good to be true. And people like to discover things for themselves, so it is better to under-sell. From a buyer's angle one must dare to be a Daniel and to float one's bread on the waters. This same buyer, who I shall call Cliff, did very well on other occasions in buying things that were either blighted or had just missed their selling occasion for some reason or other. Cliff is not the dealer's real name, but I got to know him quite well.

On another occasion we had a number of stained-glass windows that had been taken from redundant London churches that had suffered bomb damage. They had all been remade to the original vidimus designs by Edward Burne-Jones and included the pharaoh's daughter Miriam leading a dance through the River of Jordan. They were not of the period of Burne-Jones, but they were of some age and expensively made exactly to his designs. They were church-size, and that is enormous, so who is going to buy them? Try as we might we could not find a potential buyer. However Cliff bought them at a very reasonable price after the sale and had the good luck to almost immediately find an American buyer who was building a church in the United States.

Mother often found a picture she liked, but would not buy it until I had seen it. One was a large oil painting that hung in the shop of the mahogany dealers E W Cousins and Son at Ixworth, north of Bury St Edmunds. It was entitled *The Holly Seller* and was an oil painting by the northern artist Wilson Hepple. It featured an old man driving what we call in Suffolk a brumping cart that was pulled by a dickie (donkey), fully laden with holly, in a snowclad winter scene. My sister has it now. This, along with an E R Smythe of a forge in winter and other paintings, I took up to be photographed in London, where a Christmas card manufacturer agreed to give us free Christmas cards of these for allowing them to use them for their purpose.

On another occasion, Mother said that there was a snow scene picture coming up for sale at the Athenaeum in Bury St Edmunds that she liked the sound of. It was of a horse-driven sleigh coming through a forest. As it happened I was going over to our Bury office on the morning of the Monday that the sale was due to take place, and the viewing was in the morning only. An estate agent was holding the sale, and I went to view it amongst quite an upheaval. A brass plate on the reverse confirmed that it had been a presentation. It was modern, yet of some quality. Mother bought it against the antique dealer Ted Cousins for £36. It was signed by the artist F S Coburn, a Canadian and quite important artist as we were to find out, so she decided to sell it, realising £1,500. She always had a golden touch, did my mum.

We had a call one day from a gentleman of the landed gentry who had a large agricultural estate just into Essex. He had been educated at a major public school and somehow purposely showed it in all he did. He lived on his own and the word was that his family had made their money in the north of England in 'soap'! The first time that I

215

went to see him I was five minutes late for my appointment. A lady member of his staff answered the door and said that he had to go to another appointment and his instruction had been would I wait in the hall. About two hours later he came back, and I apologised to him for my being five minutes late. I felt that he had taken his time on purpose for me daring to be late for him. It all seemed a game for him to intimidate in this way.

Anyhow, I went to see him another time, for which I was of course on time. His technique was to show you certain pieces, which were usually silver plate, but occasionally the odd good painting, saying, "What will you get for this?" which, of course, put you right on the spot and you had to be accurate. After we had gone through six or seven pieces, he would tell you which he was sending or alternatively which he was going to keep as future wedding presents.

He had made for himself a bit of a reputation for his style when he phoned one day saying, "Do you play tennis?" to which I duly replied "poorly." "Oh! That's all right," he said, then asked me up to the big house for a tennis party. I could not sleep I was so scared. I had seen some of his friends and their Rolls-Royces and later for peace of mind I had to bare my soul in telling him as politely as I could that I could not make it. He seemed to pleasantly understand my social ineptness.

Another time I had been asked to go and see him as he had more saleroom potential goods. When it was time to depart we agreed that I would transport certain things in my car. Now, at that time my garage at home was full of clients' furniture awaiting sale, being fully insured of course, so my car had stood outside all night and this cold morning had about three inches of snow on the roof. I cleared the windscreens, jumped in and duly arrived at the big house on time. After I had appraised the goods in the usual way he said, "Now you take the two prints and the Georgian yew-wood tea caddy, you see, it's in perfect condition with its original key, you see don't you, and

I shall come along behind with the other pieces." "Yes thank you," I said and proceeded to the car with both hands full. To open the back door I gently rested the tea caddy, which he thought so much of, on the snow-clad roof whilst I opened the back door, when all of a sudden there came a loud 'plop'. The snow where it touched the roof had melted, causing the catastrophic mishap of the snow and tea caddy falling onto the snow-covered roadway. "What's happened, what's happened?" he said as he approached from behind. Then as he dusted down his tea caddy which he had retrieved from the snow-covered ground he mournfully said, "Oh dear, oh dear, I would rather not have had this." Leaving him mortally offended at my faux-pas, I duly left the scene and on returning to the office told the tale to my secretary who knew about him and as expected she split her sides with laughter. After that if anything went wrong at the office you could bet that someone would come out with "Oh dear, oh, dear, I would rather not have had this," in an offended public school accent.

One day he told me about how his friend Peter Scott had phoned him from an airport to go and collect him, no doubt from some wild duck sojourn. He then showed me in a book on an inside fly page, a watercolour of a rising duck inscribed 'To Julian from Peter'.

I saw him again after this when I had already decided to retire. I was purposely about five minutes late as I wanted to hear what he would say, and as expected his housekeeper told me that he had to go but would be in the garden. I exchanged winks with the old gardener in his potting shed as I approached to get my usual lecture. I saw him about a year after I had retired when both of us were viewing a local sale and he said to me, "You are sadly missed," which in its own way meant a lot, for although we had discreetly treated him as a bit of a joke his heart was in the right place if you stripped back the veneer.

In reflecting on the more interesting things that we had sold, I personally love those items that had originated during the reign of Elizabeth I. She is immensely important to our history, and her aides, the adventurers Raleigh and Drake, kept the Spanish at bay, thus there were no wars on our soil. The Virgin Queen as she was called reigned from 1558 until 1603, and these 45 years gave us a peace that brought great cultural appreciation in a return to the courts, dancing and sociality, a deep appreciation of food, arts and gaming. From the new-found Americas came turkeys and tobacco. In the saleroom this manifested in items influenced by the Renaissance, which, starting in Italy, reached England during this period just before it petered out.

The deeper appreciation of the art form of furniture making manifested in a greater decoration of furniture, to bring typical things such as gadrooning and inlay. Gadrooning is the raised rounded strips of oak that run horizontal down bulbous table legs which in this Elizabethan period particularly occurs on draw leaf tables, one of which we sold for £15,000. It had a walnut top but had some restoration. Later we sold another for £20,000, that I have already mentioned herein. We also sold several similarly decorated court cupboards, the highest price for same being £15,000. Also full tester beds and over-mantles, all with this gadrooned and inlaid decoration.

In this period, the craftsmen were not so mechanised as later and this is given away by the use of more ancient tools such as the 'froe' and an 'adze'. The froe or riving iron as it is sometimes called is made for splitting timber. It is ideal for a hurdle maker as it has a handle at right angle to the blade so that it can be hit with a hammer on the top of the blade whilst being held steady with the other hand. Riving comes from the word riven and froe from timber that has been thrown meaning split. I love to see it, as in the words of Christopher Dresser, it is putting "utility before beauty".

About 50 years ago I bought a late-Elizabethan oak mule chest that I feel is typical, in that the front has three incised arched panels above a drawer beneath with incised guilloche carving and a two-panel lid, but the exterior of the back is made entirely of timber that is thrown. By that I mean incised with a riving iron then split into usable pieces.

It is undoubtedly an acquired perception, but I love the back as much as the front for its economy and that it qualifies the piece as being Elizabethan. It has no incised inlay as have most chests of this period which are usually decoration with inlay of the darker bog oak and the lighter but equally as dense holly.

One day an item arrived in our saleroom that I think typifies this settled Elizabethan period of British culture, in the form of a cased set of Elizabethan roundels. These formed 12 circular platters upon which there was a stylised painted decoration on one side, where the pudding course of marchpane (now called marzipan) would be placed. When this had been devoured these small circular platters would be turned over to reveal a game. The set that we sold were decorated with proverbs and amusing sayings, which would have been humorous to the assembled company, but I have heard of other sets that were made up of singing games, all handwritten on these round objects. This was to give the name roundels and round-a-lay in singing. Although in this era there would be minstrels – this was of course largely a period of self-entertainment and the thought of the company, having feasted, sitting around and all taking part in this expression of self I find awe-inspiring.

Another historical thing that I found intriguing in local history is the Hanseatic League, which was a trading agreement with certain North European ports mainly in the Germanic, Baltic and North Sea ports around in the sixteenth century. This manifested in international trading warehouses, particularly in King's Lynn in Norfolk where there were large Hanseatic warehouses erected for this purpose. From an old dealer in King's Lynn I was to inspect a massive copper weathervane of a sailing ship, heeled over now and covered in green verdigris, which tells its own romantic tale. The whole east coast area had associations with other countries fronting the North Sea, particularly Holland, with Dutch people coming here for trading fairs. Hence eighteenth-century Dutch delft pieces still turn up in local auction sales, with English names on them. Seamen would likewise visit the port of Riga where there grows a particular type of Baltic birch tree, whose timber never seems to dry out so it made excellent pocket tobacco containers, and it seemed as though every seaman who ever went to the Nordic port had one. I had never seen one and was told what they were when we sold one in our saleroom.

In the early 1990s I became aware that there was now a thing called a digital image and that methods in terms of printing and the internet were going to bring changes. As mentioned, changes in technology had put our estate agency on the map in the mid-1960s when we had bought our own offset litho print machine, print maker, and Polaroid Land Camera to produce black and white photos of all particulars. On becoming aware that a car sales magazine was now issuing a digital camera to their salesmen to call and take coloured photographs of vehicles for sale to be printed in their magazine, I made contact with them. The salesman was very explicit and helpful. Our new digital camera was called a Canon Ion, and it cost just under £2,000. I also bought a new pc that was capable of downloading these pictures, and after a few teething troubles now advertised that a colour photograph of every lot would be printed in colour in our catalogue.

We also acquired Quark the printers' software along with Photoshop and Illustrator and we were the first auctioneers in the country to do this. Once again, embracing new technology had paid off. The internet however was not so advanced and our first attempt at putting a coloured photo of every lot on the internet cost us, through an agent, £2,000. At the time it was possible to envisage auction sales on the internet, and that they would come sooner or later. It really was the cutting edge of change. I waited for my son George to come into the firm with me and although he was brilliant at technology he preferred to become a DJ of modern techno music and moved to Barcelona, where I am told that this way-out music is more appreciated. He did take me to see his local football team who are reckoned to be pretty good.

With our new techno camera we could photograph almost anything, anywhere, whereas before this we had converted a store-room to a special studio with both side and overhead lighting and background. I very much believed in the power of the visual and before this we had photographed almost everything outside at my home in all weathers, having someone to hold three whiteboards to blot out the background. I can remember, with snow on the ground, warming the crew up by taking out coffee with rum in it.

We presented our first catalogue with a photograph of every lot, and later two other auctioneers quizzed me about what we were doing. One a dealer from the north of England who was to take over the running of an existing saleroom told me that he was going to follow us to the tee. He was too far away to be a competitor so I helped him all that I could. We were to use this new world system to great advantage in our next adventure.

CHAPTER 16

Wartime: 10 Shillings in the
Hat for the Red Cross

N igel and his wife Chris Oakley owned Rede Hall Farm Park, near Bury St Edmunds, with Suffolk horses, sheep and large black pigs. They ran Open Days. After much discussion I said that if we saved up suitable items would it be possible for us to hold a 1940s farm sale at his premises. Nigel was always telling stories, and had been out a few times with 'The Bumpstead Boys', an entertaining outfit of old codgers such as yours truly, generally entertaining in rural fashion in local village halls. As they lived only about three miles from Silver Ley, where Adrian Bell had farmed, and most things that we were to sell were from the war years or before, we decided to call it '1940s Farm Sale, In Adrian Bell Country'.

Adrian Bell's son Martin, the BBC presenter, kindly provided a few photos of his father for the catalogue and also gave a book to be sold for charity. It was remarkable how things came together. A vendor from Moulton Hall, near Newmarket, was most cooperative, letting us put in a number of suitable things, including three nineteenth-century oil paintings of 'naive' square cows, two of which were snapped by a London gallery specialising in naive art; a good nineteenth-century brass milk churn that held 12 gallons; a period Land Rover; and other items. I remember driving the Land Rover which scared me by wandering all over the road. My Grain and Chalk employer Peter Grain had driven one and used to steer with his knees whilst filling this pipe with his favourite tobacco – Bacon's 5081. Bacon's stood on the corner of Rose Crescent to the market square and were the old Cambridge tobacco shop with massive Scottish tobacco figures, and every mixture of tobacco under the sun.

In the sale we also had the horsedrawn farm equipment of the TV presenter, Paul Heiney, who was giving up keeping Suffolk horses. The contents of a private bygone museum, including two nineteenth-century iron man traps, an eighteenth-century hood of bells by Robert Wells of Aldbourne and also a rare nineteenth-century armorial horse brass, which realised £400. Other items from Albion House, Eye, sold well, as did most items. There was a Georgian mahogany barometer, rare in that it was by a Haverhill maker, and a pair of percussion pocket pistols in a fitted mahogany case that was inscribed Bendyshe Walton, Haverhill, and dated 1847. Walton apparently was a baker. We also sold a World War Two sheepskin flying jacket, and a World War Two Willys Jeep, plus a 1940s Allis-Chalmers tractor and a Standard Fordson one too. To complete the sale we had livestock in the form of a Suffolk mare, a yearling Red Poll bull, a trio of Norfolk horned sheep, large Black Suffolk pigs and trio of Norfolk black turkeys, making 345 lots in all. I also sold my Mother's double barrel hammerless .410 shotgun. She used to keep Silkie bantams, and had been troubled by rats, but being a farmer's daughter she knew how to use a shotgun and had killed 25 rats with 25 shots from her bedroom window. I had bought this gun for her from Mr Guiver the agricultural contractor from Stoke by Clare, who was emigrating to Australia. It was stamped ELG for the Liege Gun company of Belgium, and had badly pitted barrels, which Mac Taylor the gunsmith from Sudbury sent away to have them lapped, and which took a minute skin off the inside of the barrels. This had made it near perfect. At £150 I thought it was quite cheap, but it had to go.

A load of people dressed up for the day with a lot wearing period outfits, such as dressed as land army girls, and there were others in wartime army and nurses clothing. There was also someone dressed as a village policeman in 1940s period clothes who said it was out of Adrian Bell's book *Corduroy*. His outfit was complete with domed helmet to match. I am pleased to report that not once did he have to blow his whistle.

I wore a large Lincoln Bennett trilby hat of the prewar period and a suit that I had bespoke made in Suffolk horseman style with horseshoe buttons. I started the sale with the announcement, "I have just listened to the BBC morning news on the wireless read by Alvar Lidell, who reported, 'Several German planes have flown over the Home Counties during the night and having missed their target were made to drop their bombs at random and this was followed by the usual patter from Lord Haw-Haw who interjected that random had been heavily bombed'."

My mate Steve Monk was the head porter and when we sold a melodeon he took it out of its box and gave the assembled company a tune, which seemed to gee up the buyer who was bidding on the phone from Ireland. At the celebration in the barn afterwards, whilst another friend played, the Music Monkey as we called him got up and entertained us all with a Suffolk stepdance. The company went on to sing the wartime songs, Vera Lynn's 'The White Cliffs of Dover' and 'We'll Meet Again', Anne Shelton's 'Coming in on a Wing and a Prayer' and finishing with 'When the Lights Go On'. There was the very latest jitterbug dancing, banter and much 1940s-style fun was had by all.

The most interesting thing in the whole of this wartime reenactment however, was the sale of the Lister 1.5 H P stationary engine, which the vendor, Roy Haylock, had bought from the stockists Choppens of

Saffron Walden for £22. 10 shillings in 1943. He gave it on the understanding that the wartime control price applied. As it would have been
against the law to sell it for more than the new price of £22.10 shillings,
on reaching this price there was, as hitherto, a draw. Anyone wishing to
purchase it at this price would then have put their name on a ten-shil-
ling note (now £5) to be put in the auctioneer's hat. The winner would
then have the right to buy it at the original purchase price. All of the
money in the hat would then be sent on to the Red Cross to buy food
parcels for our prisoners-of-war. This we duly did. When the draw was
made I found it had been won by my wife, Hazel, so on her behalf I gave
it back, with the new purchase money adding to that going to the Red
Cross, which received a handsome cheque. What a friend we had in
Roy Haylock who was inspired to provide this great reenactment of the
wartime history that he had played a part in. Roy was always a Boardmans supporter and used to attend all of our farm sales. Many people
loved this bygone reenactment sale, and we were asked to do another.
I had enjoyed the day immensely but this sale was for me to be the one
that the cobbler threw at his wife – the last.

Thank you for getting thus far, I hope that you have enjoyed
sharing my adventure.